Theatre in the
Age of Kean

Drama and Theatre Studies

GENERAL EDITOR: KENNETH RICHARDS
ADVISORY EDITOR: HUGH HUNT

Also in this series:

British Theatre, 1950–70
ARNOLD P. HINCHLIFFE

The Scandinavian Theatre:
A Short History
FREDERICK AND LISE-LONE MARKER

Theatre in Ireland
MICHEÁL Ó HAODHA

Theatre in the Age of Garrick
CECIL PRICE

The Theatre of Goethe and Schiller
JOHN PRUDHOE

A Short History of
Scene Design in Great Britain
SYBIL ROSENFELD

The Edwardian Theatre
J. C. TREWIN

JOSEPH DONOHUE

Theatre in the Age of Kean

Rowman and Littlefield
Totowa, New Jersey

First published in the United States 1975
by ROWMAN AND LITTLEFIELD, Totowa, N.J.
© *Basil Blackwell 1975*

Library of Congress Cataloging in Publication Data

Donohue, Joseph W   1935–
    Theatre in the age of Kean.

    'Drama and theatre studies)
    Bibliography: p.
    Includes index.
    1. Theater—England—History.   2. English
drama—19th century—History and criticism.
I. Title.
PN2594.D6   792'.0942   75–11950
ISBN 0–87471–698–5

Set in Photon Baskerville
Printed and bound in Great Britain by
The Camelot Press Ltd., Southampton

For Therese

Contents

Plates

Acknowledgements

Research for this book was begun during tenure of the Annan Bicentennial Preceptorship at Princeton University and was promoted by grants from the American Council of Learned Societies, the Research Council of the University of Massachusetts, and the Henry E. Huntington Library. It is a pleasure to thank the persons and institutions that supported my work, especially Jeanne T. Newlin, curator of the Harvard Theatre Collection, her assistant Martha R. Mahard, my research assistant Roberta Rothstein, and the staffs of the British Museum, the Folger Shakespeare Library, the Henry E. Huntington Library, and the Houghton Library, Harvard University. I am grateful also to Jean Charnley and Marion Balderston for exceedingly generous hospitality and delightful conversations about the theatre past and present and to James Ellis, my colleague in the London Stage 1800–1900 calendar project, for the use of his splendid theatrical library and for much helpful advice.

The discussion of burletta in Chapter Three derives from my essay on the subject in *Nineteenth Century Theatre Research*, 1 (1973), 29–51. Thanks are made to the editors of that journal for permission to adapt it here. The letter from Kean to Elliston in Chapter Four is quoted by permission of the Harvard College Library.

J. D.

Notes

Although exact sources are indicated wherever possible, the annotation is representative rather than full. Sources frequently cited are abbreviated by author or title, as appropriate (e.g. Hazlitt; *Survey of London*). Complete citations will be found under the same head in the Bibliography. Unless otherwise indicated, the place of publication is London.

CHAPTER ONE

The Demise of Sheridan's Theatre

Early in the morning of 20 September 1808 the Theatre Royal in Covent Garden was destroyed by fire. The disaster killed twenty-three persons, demolished Handel's organ and a number of his manuscripts,[1] and left hundreds of people jobless. Financial loss faced the proprietors as well; a fresh capitalization of funds was required for a new playhouse, the old one having been insufficiently insured. Dating from 1732 and the first theatre on that ground, Covent Garden had undergone a complete interior reconstruction as recently as 1792 and so was, in a sense, only slightly older than the new Drury Lane erected in 1794. A mere sixteen years later, ignited (so it was thought) by wadding from a gun fired during a performance of Richard Brinsley Sheridan's spectacular romantic tragedy *Pizarro*, Covent Garden had become a smoking ruin in three hours.

Within a few short months a second, parallel disaster occurred at the Theatre Royal in Drury Lane. On the night of 24 February 1809 Drury Lane's proprietor, Sheridan, sat in the nearby Piazza Coffee House, stoically sipping refreshment while his fifteen-year-old theatre was vanishing in flames. Resigned to still another crisis in a calamitous public life, Sheridan replied to a friend who wondered at his calmness, 'A

---

[1] *Gentleman's Magazine*, 78 (1808), 846–847, 1038.

man may surely be allowed to take a glass of wine by his own fireside.'[2]

Characteristic as it was, Sheridan's witty aplomb could not minimize the extent of the loss, or the sharpness of its irony. Under his aegis the decaying theatre of Garrick's age had been replaced by a magnificent new edifice with a stage 'upon a larger scale than in any other Theatre in Europe'.[3] But the danger of fire reflected in the architect Henry Holland's plans had gone largely unheeded. The iron safety curtain had rusted and was removed, and the ingenious rooftop reservoirs for water were evidently not full. On the morning after the conflagration, Drury Lane's west wall appeared the solitary remnant. Occupational hazards and gross neglect had combined to deprive London theatregoers of both their regular sources of legitimate dramatic entertainment.

Depending on their pockets and tastes, enthusiasts could still go north of the city and witness nautical dramas presented in a tank of real water at Sadler's Wells, while closer in they could find equestrian entertainments at Astley's Olympic Pavilion in the Strand, or other amusements, often called 'burlettas' in the playbill, at the Sans Pareil, also in the Strand. Except for opera at the King's Theatre in the Haymarket, playgoers had little other recourse but to wait until Easter Monday, 3 April, when R. W. Elliston opened his newly leased Surrey-side theatre, the Royal Circus, with a season of melodramatic and pantomimic burlettas, or until May, when the little theatre in the Haymarket would begin another summer season of more traditional plays for those who by choice or necessity remained in town. Meanwhile, without the two major theatres to infuse it with continuous life, the legitimate drama languished for the rest of the winter in the limbo of printed text, since no other theatre could infringe on the monopoly shared by the two great patent houses.

Or so the proprietors of the two great houses appeared to think. Covent Garden, quickly rebuilt, opened its doors in

---

[2] Thomas Moore, *Memoirs of the Life of the Right Honourable Richard Brinsley Sheridan* (1825), II, 368–369.

[3] Henry Holland's MS. account, quoted in *Survey of London*, p. 49.

September 1808. Drury Lane followed suit late in 1812, but meanwhile the company took its patent to Samuel Arnold's previously unlicensed Lyceum Theatre in the Strand. There they resumed playing in June 1809 despite the Haymarket's privilege of producing the regular drama during the summer and despite the less overt, more long-range threat of the illegitimate houses then being licensed by willing magistrates for the performance of 'burletta'. The flexibility, not to say amorphousness, of this latter form of entertainment and the ingenuity of its producers would together present an increasingly formidable challenge as the early years of the nineteenth century progressed, so much so that by 1832 the ability of the two major theatres to protect their domain against the encroachment of the 'minor' playhouses had dwindled into impotence. Although a decade more would elapse before the multifarious facts of theatrical life were reflected in the law of the land, developments from the beginning of the century and even before were marked by an emergent need for a new kind of theatre and by the evident prior existence of an audience to match.

Judged by the nature of their reconstructed enterprises, however, the proprietors of the two new patent theatres were blind to the necessities and possibilities before them, so concerned were they with the protection of a financial—and cultural—investment. The scale, the opulence, everything about the huge new structures conceived by Robert Smirke and Benjamin Wyatt that rose up in Covent Garden and Drury Lane announced the presence of an exclusive, proprietary establishment, grandly conservative in idea and neoclassically decorous in taste (Plate 1). Offered the greatest opportunity for innovation since Charles II granted patented rights of performance to Davenant and Killigrew, the designers, financiers, and shareholders of the new theatres evinced a resolute opposition to change. And in doing so they betrayed an ignorance of certain values, social and cultural, on which dramatic and theatrical life may be observed to stand. That they acted for the best, so far as they could see, is undeniable. The sheer weight of theatrical and dramatic tradition, coupled 3 with heavy legal precedent, undoubtedly prevented any such men in a position to do so from reading the signs of the times. In retrospect those signs were unmistakable. So was the irony of the developing situation, for, in order to reclaim defecting audiences and reverse the trend of shrinking receipts, the managers of the major houses increasingly resorted to lures shamelessly exercised by their lesser contemporaries while tenaciously defending their right to the great plays of the past—and of the present, too, should any turn up.

These were the prevailing circumstances when, before a dispiritingly thin Drury Lane audience in January of 1814, a young actor named Edmund Kean made his debut as Shylock in *The Merchant of Venice* (Plate 2). The occasion was then and is still thought of as a revolution of a kind, a transformation overnight of the actor's art and, not so incidentally, of the fortunes of a sickly theatre. William Hazlitt, who like his fellow critics had witnessed the greatest acting of the day, could find nothing but superlatives to describe his response to Kean. 'There was a lightness and vigour in his tread,' he explained, 'a buoyancy and elasticity of spirit, a fire and animation' whose scope was far greater than the character of Shylock itself. 'In varied vehemence of declamation,' Hazlitt went on, 'in keenness of sarcasm, in the rapidity of his transitions from one tone and feeling to another, in propriety and novelty of action, presenting a succession of striking pictures, and giving perpetually fresh shocks of delight and surprise, it would be difficult to single out a competitor.'[4]

Kean's swift conquest of the stage of his day is only too familiar to students of the theatre. The vital chiaroscuro of his art soon thrust aside objections to his unclassically diminutive figure, harsh voice, and unorthodox style. A 'Romantic' actor in several senses of the term, Kean seems the visible embodiment of an idea whose time had come. In fact, however, his dominance in style and spirit over the theatre of his era remains a complex, problematic phenomenon, not simply a clear sign. His rescue of the Drury Lane treasury from imminent disaster was as spectacular as the comparable scene

4   Hazlitt, V, 179.

4

in any melodrama, but also as short-lived. Like the resilient but vulnerable heroine of its plays, the theatre was soon in difficulty again, thanks partly to Kean's intemperance but more importantly to the debilitating disease of encroachment that plagued the two legitimate houses. Again, a pointed irony emerges: the qualities of Kean's excellence better suited the illegitimate drama assaulting the fortresses of Covent Garden and Drury Lane than they did the supposedly pure generic forms of tragedy and comedy imitated on their stages. To consider Kean's debut in this light is to see in his appearance on the Drury Lane boards an emblem of the conflicting forces at work in the general theatrical environment.

Similarly, the Drury Lane Committee's decision to present this fiery, compelling actor may have an aura of abstract, collective genius about it, but in fact it reflects either a policy of piecemeal accommodation or simply reluctant acquiescence to the inevitable. Managers and other theatrical professionals had acted to conserve whatever could be salvaged from the repertoire, and the taste and mentality, of the theatre and audience of a bygone age, the age of Garrick and Sheridan. At the same time they found it compulsory, as Garrick and Sheridan did before them, to cater to the demands of an often tyrannical, usually fickle, always demonstrative audience. Sheridan, unceremoniously elbowed out of the new Drury Lane enterprise by the shareholders' wish to have nothing to do with his reputation for mismanagement, left to others a 'new *grand Imperial* and *incombustible Theatre*'[5] that still embraced ideals of the drama implicit in Sheridan's own *The School for Scandal* and *The Critic*. Products of a talent and a theatre in which virile language, exuberant wit, and honest sentiment mirrored a settled, homogeneous society, such latter-day classics grew out of a dramatic heritage reaching back through Dryden and Shakespeare to lively Romans and noble Greeks. That heritage was now in peril of surviving as a mere anachronism, or not surviving at all.

The rebuilt Covent Garden and Drury Lane, re-establishing

[5] *The Letters of Richard Brinsley Sheridan*, ed. Cecil Price (Oxford, 1966), III, 71.

in spirit a theatre of the past, were thus immediately besieged by the insurgent present. In the first instance of the conflict, the audiences that filled the 1809 Covent Garden, one of the earliest and most elegant examples of Greek Revival architecture, inaugurated the career of that edifice by riotous clamouring for 'Old Prices'. Disturbances in the theatre had long been a colourful feature of London life, but the duration and intensity of the 'O.P. Riots' signalled an issue of symbolic proportions. It might be justifiably argued that the mandarins in control of legitimate dramatic performance in London disdained to recognize the changing nature of the society on whose patronage (not really the right word) their own existence depended. In any case, they continued to regard the caparisoned horses, benevolent dogs and ponderous elephants now evident on their stages as the regrettable economic means of preserving an embattled tradition.

To understand Kean's impact, then, it is necessary to look beyond the immediate event to the disparate phenomena illuminated by that actor's meteoric appearance. Adopting this perspective we may first see, in the near distance of the previous quarter-century, a number of conditions and developments that require examination. Properly scanned, the age of Edmund Kean dawns at about the date of Kean's own birth in the late 1780s, when forces in the theatre and society at large were exerting pressures to which dramatic and theatrical art was slowly, hesitantly, beginning to respond. The end of that age—if our sense of an ending prompts us to distinguish one—occurs with Kean's death in 1833, or with the 1832 inquiry of a Select Committee of Parliament into the causes of the decline of the drama and with the passage of the First Reform Bill that same year, or, perhaps most fittingly, with the accession of Queen Victoria five years later. By 1837, at any rate, the persons and influences that were to shape the 'Victorian' theatre of the mid-nineteenth century were emerging or had already achieved some eminence.

Between these two approximate points half a century apart lies a period of shifting values in which the old and the new, the moribund and the vigorous, move together in mutual dependence and mistrust. In the theatre it is an age that commands attention for what it would become, but more so for what it was: a time when the nature of theatrical vitality became radically redefined, and when a regenerate (though now unliterary) drama reasserted its influential place in the lives of its audience.

CHAPTER TWO

The Theatre of the 1790s

The theatre, one of Britain's most enduring institutions, is a public art and a quotidian enterprise. Rooted in continuous contact with an audience, it is an art in which no practitioner alone, even the playwright, follows his work to fruition. Theatrical performance becomes a group endeavour from the moment the author enters the playhouse, manuscript in hand; and, of course, the playhouse must already be there. Moreover, theatrical performance not only articulates the playwright's vision of society but embodies a view held jointly by players and playgoers, managers and monarchs, scene dressers and 'shilling' gallery habitants. Allowing for individual differences in background, education, taste and intelligence, we must still acknowledge the justness of Doctor Johnson's familiar assertion, 'The Stage but echoes back the publick Voice'.[1]

The metaphor of an echo suggests the important mimetic place of the theatre in society. It also implies what is at bottom the theatre's cultural conservatism. Strangely, or not so strangely, the theatre perpetuates itself and at the same time nourishes the society around it by resisting change, doing what was done before, elevating mere habit to the alleged status of enlightened principle. And yet it is also wonderfully sensitive to

---

[1] 'Prologue Spoken by Mr. Garrick at the Opening of the Theatre in Drury-Lane, 1747', in R. S. Crane, ed., *A Collection of English Poems 1660–1800* (New York, 1932), p. 668.

shifts in public sympathies, tastes and mores, on occasion embracing the new and untried with a fervour and conviction that belie its dependence on the old and well established. Observed in a long historical perspective the theatre appears a dynamic, constantly modulating phenomenon, despite its seeming monolithic intransigence when viewed at short range.

The fact of gradual, almost imperceptible change is of special significance in the case of the English theatre of the last decade or so of the eighteenth century. In many important respects this theatre had scarcely altered since David Garrick's retirement in 1776 had delivered the reins of Dury Lane management into younger hands. True, both Drury Lane and Covent Garden had lately increased their capacities to accommodate more of London's increasing population, but the principles of day-to-day operation had not changed, nor had the identity and purpose of the major theatres themselves. A thriving playgoing populace gave audible nightly approval, by and large, to the performance of a tried and varied theatrical repertoire. The refurbishing of Covent Garden in 1792 and the rebuilding of Drury Lane completed in 1794 were accomplished in the expectation of even greater profits derived by perpetuating a deeply ingrained tradition, officially sanctioned by royal patent well over a century before.

There were compelling reasons for carrying on exactly as the managements of Drury Lane and Covent Garden did. Shortly after the Restoration of the monarchy in 1660, Sir William Davenant and Thomas Killigrew, dramatists and ardent courtiers, had contrived to obtain Charles the Second's approval for establishing two theatres for the exclusive performance of plays. The effect of this action on English theatrical life for over a century and a half to come is difficult to overestimate. The two patentees found themselves possessed of a valuable right to which no others had access, and they proceeded at once to exploit it, in the spirit of the intention of the patent itself. That intention, clearly, was to preserve theatrical life by regulation, at the same time removing the threat of trespass. Licensed privilege was its essence. Although the two separate and independent theatres that quickly arose

9

were designedly in competition, together they shared what amounted to a monopoly over the dramatic works of past and present whose enactment, in Charles's words, was to 'serue as innocent and harmlesse divertisement for many of our subjects'.[2]

The description may not seem an accurate one of Restoration drama, nor of Charles's own lively interest in playgoing (and players). The King's patent itself proved no less disputable. Its function soon came under challenge, and in succeeding generations the official and exclusive right to perform plays was entailed to the heirs of the original patentees and then repeatedly divided and sold and divided again.[3] By the early nineteenth century Covent Garden was operating on a special twenty-one-year licence, its patent held by others from whom the licensees were forced to purchase it, for a crippling sum. By 1832 the patent theatres had proved themselves a hopelessly inept means of preserving the monopoly originally granted a century and three quarters before. And yet, over this long period of frustration, exploitation, and intermittent chaos, one constant persisted: the evident value of possessing exclusive rights to the entertainment of a nation in its capital city.

The long possession of those rights by Drury Lane and Covent Garden had given the whole idea of performing plays a proprietary aura. The only allowed exception to their long-standing privilege occurred with the granting of a royal patent to the actor Samuel Foote to perform legitimate drama in his 'Little Theatre in the Haymarket', so called to distinguish it from the King's Theatre, the opera house, also situated in the Haymarket. Earlier in the century the smaller theatre had been the scene of many of Henry Fielding's burlesques and political satires, which at length grew virulent enough, in the opinion of the authorities, to require official detoxification. The infamous Licensing Act of 1737 which then ensued put a virtual stop to

[2] Quoted in Nicoll, I, 193n.
[3] For information summarized here I am indebted to Nicholson; Dewey Ganzel, 'Patent Wrongs and Patent Theatres: Drama and the Law in the Early Nineteenth Century', *PMLA*, 76 (1961), 384–396; and *Survey of London*.

Fielding's career as a dramatist by creating an official agency under the Lord Chamberlain for the licensing—in effect, the censoring—of all plays. The force of this legislation, combined with the already existing patents of the two major theatres of the metropolis, was that other presentations could be given, if at all, only by staying well away from the letter of the law or by deviously circumventing it.

Foote himself became accomplished at doing just that, by means of tickets sold to friends to join him in a dish of tea or chocolate while watching 'gratis' dramatic entertainment of his own devising. Unsatisfied with these pursuits, Foote at length was presented with a means to rise above them. In February 1766 he was thrown while attempting to ride the Duke of York's unmanageable horse, and his broken leg had to be amputated. In compensation, the Duke used his influence with the crown to obtain a lifetime patent for Foote to perform the legitimate drama during a summer season extending from 15 May to 15 September, when the winter theatres were customarily dark. London now had three houses designated 'Theatre Royal'.

Then, in a transaction whose features are typical of the inveterate confusion surrounding theatrical patent rights, Foote sold his patent to the sometime manager of Covent Garden, the elder George Colman. The Haymarket continued to be called 'Theatre Royal', but only by custom; Colman's position in his new enterprise was by no means permanently guaranteed by Foote's patent but assured only annually by licence from the Lord Chamberlain.[4] Between the major houses and Colman's theatre, taken over by his son George in 1790, friction was inevitable, with regard both to opening and closing dates and to the use of actors whom Colman was accustomed to hire from the major houses for his summer seasons. In effect, the year's lease on life regularly granted by the Lord Chamberlain's licence put the Haymarket on much the same legal foundation enjoyed by the 'minor' theatres that were to arise in London during the next several decades, and the Haymarket's position was already proving a similar,

[4] Colman, I, 235.

though not so extreme, annoyance to the managers of the winter houses.

The presence and posture of the Haymarket may be seen in retrospect, then, as an earnest of an impending larger conflict. Meanwhile another, even more ominous, sign appeared in another quarter. John Palmer, the original Charles Surface in Sheridan's *The School for Scandal* and a favourite comedian with audiences at both Drury Lane and the summer Haymarket, had resolved to try his fortune as a theatre manager. To this end he found sufficient financial support to erect an impressive playhouse in Wellclose Square, a district of the City near the Tower. The prospectus for the enterprise stated irrefutably that 'Eastern London contains more than Two Hundred Thousand Inhabitants' (a significant underestimate, it should be noted) and called attention to 'the many advantages arising from a well regulated and supported Theatre to its immediate neighbourhood'.[5] Indeed, the point would seem incontestable that the large populace of this part of London had as much right to a place of local entertainment as did inhabitants of the western section, where Drury Lane, Covent Garden, and the Haymarket catered to an indentifiably if not exclusively local clientele. The managements of the three Theatres Royal nevertheless rose as one to contest the legality of the enterprise—but only at the last moment, when Palmer's new structure, named with touching simplicity 'The Royalty Theatre', was about to open.

Ever since Palmer himself laid the cornerstone of his 2,500-seat theatre in 1785, he had kept secret the legal basis for his proceeding, meanwhile putting doubts to rest with the disarming self-assurance that had earned him his sobriquet of 'Plausible Jack'. A few days before the opening on Saturday, 9 June 1787, however, the managers of the three Theatres Royal caused to have published in the newspapers extracts from various acts of Parliament classifying actors as vagabonds and vagrants, and threatened to seek their enforcement against all lawbreakers. The most fearsome of these laws was undoubtedly the Licensing Act of 1737 itself, which stipulated

[5] Prospectus for the Royalty Theatre (Folger Shakespeare Library).

a fine of £50 for anyone convicted of acting for 'hire, gain, or reward' any play or theatrical performance not previously allowed by royal patent or licensed by the Lord Chamberlain.[6] Palmer had managed to attract a large and distinguished audience to his theatre, but he had not reckoned on the vindictiveness of the three other managements, who had looked on in mendacious silence for a year and a half until the Royalty was about to swing wide its doors. In desperation Palmer arranged for the proceeds of the first night to go to the benefit of the London Hospital, but it was evident he would have to close. His address to the audience on opening night revealed that the leg his enterprise stood on was no stronger than a licence from the Governor of the Tower. Small wonder he had kept his authority hidden until then, since obviously—to anyone, apparently, except the perennially sanguine Palmer himself and his luckless financial backers—it could not overrule a positive act of Parliament to the contrary.[7]

Palmer's cause, just as it really was, suffered defeat from his colossal naïveté and, in the recriminations he showered on his antagonists, his self-righteousness. Only in fantasy, perhaps, could he have been acquitted, as he was in an anonymous printed description of his 'trial' held in the Olympian Shades before the Lord Chief Justice Shakespeare. Emphasizing in mock-seriousness the legal classification of Palmer and his actors as 'rogues, vagabonds, sturdy beggars and vagrants', the account allows the erstwhile manager to plead his case himself. Palmer's testimony is weighted heavily in favour of the requirements of the theatre-going public, referring to the need for 'rational and instructing entertainments, tending to moralize and improve' the 'numerous and respectable body of his Majesty's subjects residing within the districts of the Tower and adjacent parts'. . . .[8] Such an argument, largely unvoiced in Palmer's own time, would become a strident call for change

[6] The act in question is 10 George II, c. 28 (21 June 1737).
[7] See Nicholson, p. 123 & n.
[8] *The Trial of Mr. John Palmer, Comedian, and Manager of the Royalty Theatre* . . . (1787), pp. 4, 18 (Folger Shakespeare Library).

as the years moved on into the early nineteenth century. Despite its failure to divest the other theatres of their exclusive right to the legitimate drama, the Royalty venture had a long-term effect on the fortunes of the majors by virtue of the precedent it established. Palmer's was the first serious attempt to break the monopoly, and only the first of many.

Several weeks after his abortive one-night stand, Palmer reopened the Royalty for 'theatrical entertainments' of the sort already available at Sadler's Wells, comprising pantomimes, burlettas, dances, and so on, with no spoken dialogue, thus skirting the letter of the Licensing Act. The real threat felt by the managers of the majors from even this sort of amusement is clear in the prosecution and conviction as vagrants of two of Palmer's actors who had injudiciously uttered a few words.[9] Difficult as it may be to sympathize with the ruthless behaviour of the controllers of the patent theatres and the Haymarket, who had unashamedly swallowed their differences in the face of a common enemy, it remains true that legality and precedent were on their side, however much these briefs deserved challenge. It was a triumph, however short-lived, for tradition, a reassertion of the power and prestige of the established theatre with which most Londoners, playgoers or not, were familiar.

At any given time in the history of London and its theatres the actual playgoing populace has represented a relative and somewhat vaguely defined minority. Even where evidence is sufficient for more than a guess, estimates of the exact percentage of playgoers to total population vary widely and are notoriously susceptible to error. It is of course true that, in an early development of real importance, the broadly based popular audience of Shakespeare's day had become divided, in the early seventeenth century, into two groups, attending respectively the public and private playhouses. But it is hazardous, and in fact simply wrong, to conclude that it was the privileged audience of such Jacobean and Caroline playhouses as the Blackfriars and the Phoenix whose descendants were the exclusive frequenters of Davenant's and

14   [9] Nicholson, pp. 113–114.

Killigrew's court-oriented theatres later in that century. The fact of Samuel Pepys's diary itself refutes this inference, but in addition to his own attendance at the theatre Pepys records the presence of a wide variety of persons, not just royalty, aristocracy, and gentry but merchants, authors, critics, 'cits', ladies of varied reputation, clerks, apprentices, and others. The Restoration and eighteenth-century audience was always a mixed one. If generalizations are difficult, however, several features of this audience may still be described in terms of social and cultural identity.

The most elementary fact about an audience is that it congregates in one place for purposes either aesthetic or social or, more likely, both. Riots or large-scale disruptions notwithstanding, the eighteenth-century audience was a homogeneous group, yet at the same time well aware of its own distinctive components. The basic arrangement of the traditional theatre auditorium into boxes, pit, and galleries—simultaneously an architectural and a social division—by no means created mutually exclusive seating areas. The merchant, newspaper man or respectable woman who might typically be found seated in the pit might be encountered without surprise in a box. A gentleman of fashion who really wanted to see and hear, rather than just be seen, might forsake his customary side box for the pit. The coachman or serving woman with extra money to spend could easily appear in places less distant than those provided by the second, 'shilling' gallery.

In 1809 Frederick Howard, Earl of Carlisle, described the traditional audience in a way that balances a sense of their mobility with an even greater impression of stability and decorum:

A modern audience would be surprised to hear how the public were accommodated forty years ago. The side boxes were few in number, and very incommodious, especially when the frequenters of those boxes ever appeared in them in full dresses, the women in hoops of various dimensions, and the men with swords and habiliments all calculated to deny convenient space to their neighbours. Frocks were admitted into the front boxes, but they were not usually worn by

15

gentlemen in the evening; women of the town quietly took their stations in the upper boxes, called the green boxes; and men whom it did not suit either to be at the expense of dress, or who had not time to equip themselves, as before described, resorted to the pit. This of course comprehended a large description of persons, such as belonged to the inns of court, men of liberal pursuits and professions; and who, by an uniform attendance at the playhouse, became no incompetent judges of the drama. . . . The general custom of wearing swords was certainly productive of spilling blood before resentment found time to cool; but as far as the theatre was concerned it was instrumental to decorum; the scene was hardly ever disconcerted by noisy quarrels, blows, or such indecencies as we now witness. . . . Women of the town were never permitted in the boxes below stairs with the single exception of the beautiful Kitty Fisher, whose appearance occasioned great dismay among all the frequenters, male and female, of the hitherto unpolluted front boxes.[10]

Price was by no means the only criterion, and the impression ultimately gained from contemporary accounts is of a varied, vigorous assembly whose common motive was the experience of playgoing itself and all that it entailed, but most specifically the performances by actors and actresses who called themselves 'His Majesty's Servants' but were in a real way the servants of that audience as a whole.

In this sense the audience remained the same throughout the period. Nevertheless, two important changes took place over the course of the eighteenth century. The first, easily inferred from the growing seating capacity of remodelled and rebuilt theatres, is the phenomenon of increasing size. The second, less easy to define, is the great levelling process that G. F. A. Wendeborn, a German resident of London, illustrates in *A View of England Toward the Close of the Eighteenth Century*, published in London in 1791. 'Many of the gentlemen and ladies in the boxes,' he observes, 'elegantly dressed and outwardly adorned as they are, resemble, notwithstanding, their very homely friends in the upper-gallery, who are more

[10] Frederick Howard, *Thoughts on the Present Condition of the Stage, and upon the Construction of a New Theatre* (1809), quoted by Nicholson, pp. 182–184.

taken and pleased with the outward shew of the representation than with the intrinsic value of a good play.'[11] The remark is pointed towards the lavish spectacle more and more evident on the stage at the century's end, but its clear implication is of a common identity that transcends the class 'barriers' still prevailing in ordinary social intercourse.

An example of this development of 'middle-class' attitudes and values occurs in the increasingly frequent appearance of a wealthy merchant, sympathetically treated, in the *dramatis personae* of such plays as Steele's *The Conscious Lovers* (Drury Lane, 1722–23), George Lillo's *The London Merchant* (Drury Lane, 1730–31), and Richard Cumberland's *The West Indian* (Drury Lane, 1770–71). Such evidence has been interpreted to signify the growing attraction to the playhouse of a bourgeois audience of means, but merchants frequented the theatre before Steele was born. What is evident here, rather, is the enlarging sympathetic interest of the audience as a whole in persons unrepresentative of the kings, heroes and princesses of the ideal present or legendary past. In the instance of Cumberland's comedy the hero, Belcour, is a young outlander of uncertain birth whose eventual success depends on his being acknowledged as a son by the rich and beneficent London merchant Stockwell and, finally, on the willingness of an entire audience to take this well-meaning but extravagant interloper to their hearts. One must stop short of accepting at full value the playwright's sentimental claim, in effect, of having moulded his audience into a new and healthful social unity.[12] Still, the favourable response to Cumberland's play and to others like it came from an audience increasingly conscious of the values his comedy espoused, an audience, moreover, that was thronging in significantly greater numbers to the theatre.

By the 1790s London contained some 900,000 people in Westminster, the City, and Middlesex. An informed estimate has it that, by this time, the average nightly attendance at each of the two major theatres had risen from about 1,000 at mid-

[11] II, 182, quoted by Leo Hughes, *The Drama's Patrons* (Austin, Texas, 1971), p. 179.

[12] *Memoirs of Richard Cumberland. Written by Himself* (1807), I, 274.

century to about 1,500.[13] These are approximations; accurate figures for capacity are difficult to ascertain before the last part of the eighteenth century, when detailed evidence becomes available. It is obvious none the less that the theatres were expanding their auditoria (as well as enlarging their stages), obviously with a view towards additional receipts. Even with this general trend in mind, the cavernous enormity of the 1794 Drury Lane still comes as a shock, and only somewhat less so the size of the refurbished 1792 Covent Garden. The contemporary architectural theorist George Saunders gave a capacity of 2,170 for Covent Garden as reconstructed in 1782, but in the refurbishing of only ten years later the figure had increased by almost 50 per cent to 3,013.[14] Even this great size was exceeded by the new Drury Lane. Before its demolition in 1791 the old structure had housed nearly 2,300,[15] but according to one contemporary estimate the magnificent new edifice that arose on the site could admit a total of 3,611 patrons[16]—a figure still not as high as the architect Holland's original calculation of 3,919.[17] 'At length,' rejoiced a writer in the *Morning Chronicle*, 'we have an English theatre worthy of our opulence and taste.'[18] Not just the decor, but the scale, was what he evidently had in mind. By these standards it was no wonder that the 'Little' Haymarket, with a capacity of about 1,500, was considered an intimate playhouse.

'You are come to act in a wilderness of a place,' Mrs. Siddons explained to William Dowton, making his Drury Lane debut in 1796.[19] No doubt the unprecedented enlargement of both stage and auditorium in the closing decade of the eighteenth century had an irremediable, even epoch-making,

[13] Hogan, Intro., p. ccix.

[14] Saunders, *A Treatise on Theatres* (1790), p. 87; Hogan, Intro., p. xliv.

[15] Hogan, Intro., p. xliii.

[16] *Monthly Mirror* (July 1797), cited in Hughes, *The Drama's Patrons*, p. 185.

[17] *Survey of London*, p. 52. The lower figure tends to be corroborated by the actor-manager John Philip Kemble's preliminary estimate of 3,510 persons, with corresponding receipts totalling £649. 5s.—'Memoranda of J. P. Kemble', Vol. I, f. 195, British Museum Add. MS. 31,972—a more credible figure than the £830 indicated by the *Star*, 5 May 1794.

[18] 13 March 1794.

[19] Percy Fitzgerald, *The Kembles* (1871), I, 310.

effect on the actor's art. To one observer in 1810 whose opinion can stand for the post-1790 period generally, a spectator well up in the house has the sense of actors appearing like Lilliputians. 'Not a feature of the face can be distinguished,' he complained, 'far less the variations and flexibility of the muscles, the turn of the eye and graceful action' that give energetic life to dramatic composition.[20] A still later commentator, writing near the end of Kean's career, implied that the smaller house at the Haymarket was the place to find Kean at his best, since his merits lay not at all in lofty declamation but in 'that rapid transition of passion, which is best indicated by the expression of the features, and by the gestures of the body'. Kean's success there, this writer believed, was attributable simply to the small size of the house, enabling an audience to hear every word and see every expression and at the same time requiring from the actor no more than 'a natural exertion'.[21]

The impact of relative size on the development of house specialities also becomes evident in this new age. Considerable overlapping takes place, of course, early and late in the period, in the repertoire of plays, pantomimes, and other pieces offered to London's theatregoing public by the three legitimate houses, since the actors and actresses with their familiar special talents were so often the same, winter and summer. Still, the huge stages of Drury Lane and Covent Garden, equipped with the latest and largest in scenes and machines and staffed by inventive painters and technical experts, were capable of thoroughly overshadowing the Haymarket when it came to the management of processions, pyrotechnics, real water, and spectacular delights in general; and to this they could couple their long-standing reputation for the best in old-fashioned tragedy and comedy. The smaller stage of the Haymarket, on the other hand, was well suited for presenting at close range London's most amusing players, vital and idiosyncratic, performing a substantial and appealing repertoire of native

[20] Pamphlet account of Privy Council proceedings of 16, 19 and 26 March 1810, quoted in Nicholson, p. 205.
[21] Unidentified clipping dated [June 1830] in Hawkins, III, f. 320.

dramatic art. In addition the Haymarket developed a species of musical history play that, in company with other pieces addressed to the patriotic hearts of an audience, did much to reinforce a sense of national identity during a time of protracted international crisis and political and social unrest.

Granted these important distinctions, the similarities among the three houses were nevertheless greater than their differences, for each depended on a system of performing plays that had remained unchanged for generations. The idea of a repertory theatre grows from the notion that a fresh play each night, given by a group of actors and actresses each of whom has a special line of business and is proficient in a number of roles, will provide sufficient variety to bring a large audience into the theatre week after week, month after month. But the theory of the nightly change of bill gives way in practice to a policy that regulates the length of the run by an estimate of what the traffic will bear. A resoundingly successful new play, or afterpiece, or new actor or actress, is not likely to be replaced the next night by some other production or performer out of naïve obeisance to principle. The clear implications of success are not to be argued with. All the same, the prior assumption of the manager of a repertory theatre is that success in any given form is bound not to last. With a sharp eye on the nightly receipts and (he hopes) a sensitive finger on the pulse of the public, the manager contrives to replace a waning favourite instantly with either a fresh novelty or a tried and true stock piece, or perhaps a combination of the two, since the nightly bill regularly offered both a mainpiece usually of five acts and a shorter afterpiece, sometimes more than one.

The manager could do this and, conditions being favourable, make a successful long-term practice of it because of the composition of his acting company and the existence on his prompter's shelves of an impressive stock of plays. It was not at all uncommon for an actor or actress of this period—as in periods before and after—to command thirty, forty, or more roles, any of which could be sharpened in the memory as necessary and performed on short notice, often a day or two but perhaps a quarter of an hour, in an emergency. Given such players, whose high professionalism included a typical ability at quick study, and a number of plays culled from a tradition some two centuries old and augmented by carefully chosen new pieces, a clever manager could introduce almost limitless variety into the experience of theatregoing.

Strictly speaking, every season is a law unto itself, but in so far as any one can be taken as representative, the first full season at Sheridan's new Drury Lane, under the management of the leading actor John Philip Kemble, was so. A survey of the 1794–95 season at this playhouse will illustrate the prevailing practice, together with its hazards and rewards.[22]

Of the fifty mainpieces introduced over the course of this season of 1794–95, seven were new. Evidently, the insertion of fresh mainpieces into the repertory was a shrewdly calculated operation, new works being spread out over almost the entire season at intervals of about one month. Two of the new plays appeared before Christmas, in late October and December, followed by one each in February, March and April and the final two, only a week apart, in May. Of these seven, two were unequivocal triumphs, while several more became moderately successful and two failed utterly.

The first success of the season was a comic opera, *The Cherokee*, by James Cobb, a specialist in this form of entertainment and a veteran of some fifteen years as a comic dramatist for Drury Lane. Introduced on 20 December, *The Cherokee* amassed a record of sixteen performances by 19 February, its last appearance of the season. Yet, successful as it seemed to be, this opera reappeared for only a single performance the next season and then dropped out of the repertory. During the period of its popularity no other new mainpiece was allowed to detract from it, but no sooner did *The Cherokee* begin to fall off than another fresh play appeared, this one destined for enduring renown. Richard Cumberland's

---

[22] The following survey could not have been made without the full and accurate calendar of performances for the last quarter of the century compiled by Hogan in *The London Stage 1776–1800*. (See *The London Stage 1660–1800*, cited in note 38 below.)

serious comedy *The Wheel of Fortune* made its debut on 28 February with Kemble in the central role of the stern-browed misanthrope Penruddock, a character whose wounded dignity and inveterate hauteur exactly suited this actor's style. The eighteen performances achieved by this production were only the beginning of a success that lasted well into the early nineteenth century, the role of Penruddock remaining one of Kemble's most valuable possessions. Nor was this the only instance of Cumberland's contribution this season to the coffers of the Drury Lane treasury. The last new mainpiece this year, Cumberland's sentimental comedy *First Love*, opened on 12 May and played intermittently for eight performances into June. Although it never achieved the lasting popularity of *The Wheel of Fortune*, it did catch fire for seventeen performances in 1795–96 and appeared occasionally for two seasons after.

Otherwise, plaudits for authors of full-length works this season remained elusive. Joseph Berington's *Emilia Galotti*, adapted from the well-known tragedy by the German playwright G. E. Lessing, lasted only three nights from its debut on 28 October; and, despite the popularity of the form itself, James Hook's comic opera *Jack of Newbury* fared only slightly better, with five performances beginning 6 May. In the previous month, on 17 April, the sole produced comedy of Edward Jerningham, *The Welch Heiress*, appeared once and was then summarily withdrawn 'at the Desire of the Author'.[23] But the most unqualified disappointment must have been the failure of *Edwy and Elgiva* by Madame D'Arblay—the celebrated novelist Fanny Burney—on 21 March. Advertised as a tragedy, it proved merely a disaster, keeping the audience 'in the height of good humour, by frequent irresistible claims on their risible faculties'.[24] Even the ponderous histrionic talent of Mrs. Siddons, who played the fated heroine Elgiva, could not prevent the assembly from laughing through her death scene.[25]

The fate of afterpieces on the Drury Lane stage during the 1794–95 season was similarly unpredictable. Coincidentally, as

[23] Hogan, III, 1746.
[24] *Morning Herald*, 23 March, quoted in Hogan, III, 1738.
[25] Hogan, III, 1739.

in the case of the mainpieces, there were seven new afterpieces out of the total of forty performed. On 1 November appeared a highly successful farce by the prolific comic dramatist and later anthologist Elizabeth Inchbald. *The Wedding Day* entertained audiences nineteen times this season and went on to become a staple of the repertory, but another farce, *Nobody*, by Mary Robinson, held for only three performances beginning 29 November and then vanished. February then proved the month of success for Drury Lane. After some fifty-four rehearsals,[26] a spectacular three-act pantomime entitled *Alexander the Great; or, The Conquest of Persia* burst forth in all its panoramic splendour and captivated playgoers for some thirty-six performances. Its inventor (the word 'author' seems quite inadequate) was James Harvey D'Egville, a dancer and currently the ballet master at the King's Opera in the Haymarket. The playbill pointedly described *Alexander* as 'a Representation calculated to shew the extent and powers of the New Stage'.[27] Nor was the attraction confined to the sudden transformation of scenes or the glinting panoply of a host of human actors. A genuinely new addition had arrived. Alexander's car, which had not been completed in time for opening night, was sent on at the second performance 'drawn by two elephants, and accompanied by Darius' car, drawn by three white horses'. In comparison with this great novelty, a trophy-laden car pulled by soldiers and 'covered with burnished gold and silver' must have seemed almost routine.[28] It is noteworthy that, for all the expense and effort devoted to this enterprise, *Alexander* was not repeated the next season. Typical of the lavishly executed pantomimes of the period, which rapidly became regular holiday attractions introduced immediately after Christmas, it disappeared for ever once its novelty had dwindled.

There was nothing to equal *Alexander*'s conquest in the rest of the season, certainly not in other afterpieces. A musical farce

[26] Hogan, III, 1728.
[27] Playbill for 10 February 1795, quoted by Hogan, III, 1727.
[28] Notes of William Powell, Drury Lane prompter, quoted by Hogan, III, 1728.

by Samuel Birch and Thomas Attwood, *The Adopted Child*, attained a fair hearing for six performances, beginning in early May, and found a small place in the repertoire for at least five seasons thereafter. And an anonymous entertainment called *A Musical Olio*, which opened the next night after *The Adopted Child*, held for just one showing but reappeared twice the following year. At the end of May, two final novelties emerged, their nature and reception reflecting an important facet of the relationship between audience, actor and dramatist. The actor John Whitfield, like the other members of the company, was allowed a benefit for which, instead of an established role from the repertory, he chose an interlude of his own devising. The result was *A Masonic Melange*, and to all appearances it served its restricted purpose. The final new piece also played only once, though not intentionally. John Peter Roberdeau's satire *Saint Andrew's Festival; Or, The Game at Goff* 'found the audience in so ill a humour that it was soon put an end to by a general condemnation of it'.[29]

The unforecastable fortunes of a repertory season become immediately evident in accounts of this kind, but it is necessary to remember that new pieces, regardless of their success, are statistically only a minor part of the season's attractions. The new mainpieces of the 1794–95 season comprised merely 14 per cent of the total number of mainpieces, while the afterpieces accounted for only a slightly higher portion, 17.5 per cent, of their group. The established plays of the repertoire, whether as old as Shakespeare and Massinger or as new as Sheridan and Cumberland, were the ones depended on to carry the season through to a net financial success, provided of course that the manager was skilful enough in manipulating this repertoire, had the full co-operation of his acting company and supporting staff, was not too heavily beset by illness, the plague of the repertory system, and retained the coveted patronage of the public.

Given these favourable, not to say miraculous, conditions, one of the most conspicuous causes of the repertory company's success lies in the enduring popularity of the authors whose

[29] *European Magazine* (June 1795), p. 414, quoted by Hogan, III, 1760.

plays appear again and again, year after year. Although Shakespeare's position was not always so high, by the late eighteenth century he had cleanly outdistanced his former chief competitors Beaumont and Fletcher and Ben Jonson. While the former pair are represented this season with one play, *The Chances*, and Jonson not at all, Shakespeare contributes no fewer than nine titles to the Drury Lane season's total of seventy-five mainpieces, and these nine are played for some twenty-five performances; on the average, one night in every eight. The most frequent play is *Macbeth*, set before the public the previous April in a new and lavish mounting as the first dramatic offering in the new theatre. Its seven performances are nearly equalled by the five of Kemble's new production of *Measure for Measure*, Mrs. Siddons playing Isabella to Kemble's Duke (Plate 3). Among the rest are the comedies *As You Like It*, *Twelfth Night* and *All's Well That Ends Well*, the histories of *Henry V*, *Henry VIII* and *King John*, and one other tragedy, *Othello*.

Next to Shakespeare in this Drury Lane season is not Otway (although that dramatist's reputation holds well into the nineteenth century)[30] but Sheridan. Not surprisingly, every one of Sheridan's plays written to this date appears for at least one performance, with the sole exception of *St. Patrick's Day; The Critic* is, as usual, played as an afterpiece. At this point, the list of authors and plays begins to indicate another, less happy aspect of the repertory system: the difficulty a new writer evidently has of breaking into the ranks of established playwrights. Other than Sheridan, the only contemporary authors blessed with the production of one or more plays at Drury Lane this year (other than the new works previously discussed) are Cumberland, with *The Jew*, the first sympathetic treatment of its subject on the English stage; James Cobb, the reliable comic opera man, represented by his Gothic musical *The Haunted Tower*; and the younger George Colman, whose highly successful drama *The Mountaineers*, produced at the Haymarket, was brought forward at Drury Lane in October for

---

[30] See Aline M. Taylor, *Next to Shakespeare: Otway's* Venice Preserv'd *and* The Orphan *and Their History on the London Stage* (Durham, N.C., 1950).

eight performances. The plight of the contemporary dramatist vividly appears in assessing the competition offered by the traditional authors represented this year: in addition to Shakespeare and Beaumont and Fletcher, there are Congreve, Southerne, Vanbrugh, Farquhar, Rowe, Centlivre, Cibber and Gay, all present in the repertoire for over sixty years—a daunting list, but augmented by such stalwart dramatists of the middle and late eighteenth century as Garrick, Whitehead, Moore, Home, Philips, and Murphy. What little chance an unknown author had in assaulting so well defended a fortress seems clear enough.

And yet it remains true that new and untried authors came forward with noticeably greater frequency as the late eighteenth century gave way to the early nineteenth. The fact reflects not only the growth of the minor theatres and the insatiable hunger of majors and minors alike for whatever novelties might please an omnivorous public, but also the perennial attraction of the theatre itself.

No one, it seems safe to say, has ever explained that attraction satisfactorily. The mixed fortunes of the 1794–95 season at Drury Lane are typical of the theatre generally, not just of the theatre of this decade. Although Drury Lane ended the season in the black, the profits were by no means enormous, nor is it unusual to find this so despite the apparent novelty of a new and elegant playhouse in its first full season. Moreover, nothing in the calendar for Covent Garden this same year controverts the general impression of the uncertain dividends paid, in any quarter, on theatrical investment. Chance governs so much in the day-to-day operation, the pitfalls are so many, potential success so often evaporates before the fact or goes sour afterwards, that persons foolhardy enough to risk association with the theatre seem cause for wonder, or ridicule. Yet, paradoxically, many lives are happily (or miserably) spent in the train of the theatre's irresistible fascination, often, if not always, in this period, with one goal in mind: London, and Covent Garden or Drury Lane. For those with hearts and fortunes almost religiously committed to this most unstable vocation, London remained the traditional mecca. But the actors and actresses who finally walked that ground came from a theatre that comprised a tradition of its own: the theatre of the provincial cities and, in many cases, of the smaller settlements in between, to which itinerant players journeyed, following ancient precedent, in perpetual hope of tolerant officials, full auditoriums, dry beds, and, in time, a permanent playhouse.

The provincial theatre of the British Isles remains a subject of great interest but one not yet graced by as much attention as it deserves. Unfortunately, though perhaps inevitably, theatrical activity outside London has tended to remain in the shadow of life in the chief metropolis, except of course to the people who live in the provinces and find entertainment, or a livelihood, there. The danger in describing the nature of provincial playhouses is to see them entirely as schools for later greatness, purveyors of the cream of their hard-won crop to the London stage. This bias may be understandable in view of the fact that no other sort of school was available to a young man or woman who had ultimate designs on London audiences. George Frederick Cooke became widely known as a formidable, eccentric portrayer of Shakespearean and other villains, not because of the twenty years he spent in Manchester, Newcastle, Chester and elsewhere, but because of a subsequent period half that long spent before the audiences of London. The playbill for Kean's London debut identified the unknown actor as being 'from the Theatre Royal, Exter' (*sic*), an identity soon outgrown and silently discarded.[31] 'Exter' was simply Kean's most recent temporary home before he was finally 'discovered' and engaged for Drury Lane. The London mentality could be shamefully neglectful of provincial life, so much so that mention of such origins in the bill would seem useful only to announce the ultimate destination of an offending player.

Still another partial truth about provincial theatre requires scrutiny. In the London off-season, roughly from June to

[31] Playbill for Drury Lane, 26 January 1814 (Harvard Theatre Collection). For Kean's touring in Wales prior to his London debut, see Cecil Price, *The English Theatre in Wales in the Eighteenth Century* (Cardiff, 1948), pp. 97–100.

September, although this varied and tended to become shorter as time went on, unemployed actors and actresses might be hired for the summer season at the Haymarket if they were talented and well known. For many years, however, the alternative had existed of a contract of some weeks in Dublin, Edinburgh, Bristol or some other city that supported a theatre (sometimes more than one, as in Dublin and Edinburgh) and provided audiences eager for a glimpse of a star from London. Mrs. Siddons, Kemble, Mrs. Jordan, Cooke, Kean—the list could go on and on of actors and actresses who took themselves to the provinces once the summer had come. Moreover, some of the lesser London players formed troupes for annual visits to cities such as Canterbury, Liverpool and Ipswich. It should be unnecessary to add that at least some provincial theatres were not seasonal or merely summer playhouses but year-round operations. As important as the relationship was between the theatres in the outlying country and those in London, their primary, and long-term, significance must be seen in light of their contribution to the life and culture of the local community.

A measure of their evident importance to the localities in which they thrived, or languished, may be found in the increasing number of playhouses allowed to designate themselves as Theatres Royal. By 1800 royal patents had been granted to Bath, Bristol, Cheltenham, Chester, Cork, Dublin, Edinburgh, Hull, Liverpool, Manchester, Margate, Newcastle-upon-Tyne, Norwich, Richmond (Surrey), Weymouth, Windsor, York,[32] Aberdeen[33] and Yarmouth.[34] Additional patents issued after the turn of the century included those for Kingston (1803), Birmingham (1807),[35] Edinburgh (a second theatre, 1809), Dundee (1810) and Perth (1820).[36] Legally the designation was of great advantage, of course, because it gave the official sanction of the monarch to the performance of

[32] Hogan, Intro., p. cxxviii.
[33] Nicoll, IV, 233.
[34] Nicoll, IV, 238.
[35] Nicholson, p. 139n.
[36] Nicoll, IV, 235–238.

spoken drama. Of greater importance is the effect this privilege had on the lives of provincial audiences, who, like their London counterparts, could now see on a more regular and secure basis a living heritage of dramatic art performed by their own local repertory company and, on occasion, by a superb actor or actress down from London. They also had the unique advantage of watching a young player grow, approaching a demanding role like Othello, Jane Shore, Macheath or Rosalind with increasing competence and self-assurance. The audiences of the Bath-Bristol circuit had that happy fortune in the case of the young Sarah Siddons before London audiences could connect the name with the inexperienced, unsatisfactory girl so terrified of acting at Garrick's Drury Lane that she had failed there in her little-noticed London debut performances in 1775–76. Moreover, some few provincial managers like Tate Wilkinson of York enjoyed the enviable reputation of having prepared a long line of actors and actresses for the London stage who then returned to act for him regularly over their careers, while at the same time having built a loyal if not always numerous audience in the towns that comprised his annual circuit.[37]

The importance, then, of the provincial theatres themselves and their contribution to the theatre of Britain as a whole must be granted. Attention nevertheless returns inevitably to London, its theatres, its players and its audiences. And as the eighteenth century gives way to the nineteenth, changes in the nature of the theatre, and consequently in the drama, require detailed assessment. A calendar of performances for this capital city in the eighteenth century can be devoted essentially to the three structures that housed the legitimate drama.[38] Adopting the same focus for the early nineteenth century

[37] Although Wilkinson spent four full months playing in York, he managed in a year's time to take his company to theatres in Leeds, Pontefract, Wakefield, Doncaster and Hull—Charles Beecher Hogan, 'One of God Almighty's Unaccountables: Tate Wilkinson of York', in *The Theatrical Manager in England and America*, ed. Joseph W. Donohue, Jr. (Princeton, 1971), p. 84n.

[38] See Emmett L. Avery *et al.*, *The London Stage 1660–1800*, 5 parts in 11 vols. (Carbondale, Ill., 1960–68).

would introduce a gross distortion of the facts. In this new age the three Theatres Royal become as much a point of departure as a locus of interest. Genuine importance lies in the all too evident difficulties encountered by the major and minor theatres in attempting to develop an enduring repertoire, and in the bitter internecine struggles that ensued. An account of the history of this conflict, and of the place of actor and actress in it, forms a necessary preliminary to a study of the drama of the time itself.

CHAPTER THREE

The Theatre
of the Early 1800s

A coherent history of the London theatre in the early
nineteenth century could be outlined simply by listing the
structures devoted to theatrical performance that existed at the
end of the eighteenth century and the new buildings that grew
up among them. There is much to be said for the view that the
drama cannot be fully understood apart from the history of the
theatres in which it is enacted. The play script and theatre
building are true potentialities only with reference to each
other, however interesting they remain when scrutinized
separately. No wonder, then, that the physical theatre itself
assumes such importance in the history of the art. Not only
does it provide the place where the essential activity occurs but,
by virtue of its form, at once architectural and social, it defines
the nature of that activity and shapes the audience's response.

During the half-century prior to Victoria's accession in 1837
an unprecedented number of theatres in London and across
the Thames in Surrey were built, rebuilt or extensively
refurbished, some more than once. Their history forms a
primary part of the present chronicle.

After Palmer's ill-directed enthusiasm produced the Royalty
Theatre in 1787, the 1790s saw a series of new theatres emerge.
In 1791 the new opera house, the King's Theatre in the
Haymarket, opened its doors, the previous structure having
succumbed to fire in 1789. In this same year of 1791 two other

theatres, the King's Theatre (Pantheon) and the Sans Souci, came into existence. The Pantheon, intended as an opera house, burned down less than a year later, and although a second building arose in 1795 it was used chiefly as a place of assembly until converted to theatrical use and opened in 1812—only to be partly burned towards the end of that same year. After another brief life in 1813–14 as the English Opera House (Pantheon), it fell into decay. The Sans Souci, in contrast, remained uncharred for the length of its career. In 1791 the elder Charles Dibdin built this theatre in the Strand near Southampton Street and, fortified with a five-year licence from the Lord Chamberlain, began there his one-man musical entertainment *Private Theatricals; or, Nature in Nubibus*, continuing in this vein until 1796. Meanwhile, he erected a second theatre of the same name on a new site, which opened in 1796 with another series of one-man entertainments. After Dibdin's retirement in 1804 the Sans Souci remained in use sporadically until 1807.[1]

Meanwhile, the refurbishing of Covent Garden in 1792 was followed by the completion of the new Drury Lane in 1794. In contrast, the little Haymarket, remodelled and slightly enlarged by the elder Colman on taking over Foote's theatre in 1776, remained intact until 1821, when a new structure was built slightly south of the old one as part of John Nash's remodelling of London.[2] In this same period of the 1790s there also existed several theatres, called 'minor' to distinguish them from the houses where the 'major' repertory of legitimate drama was played, whose origins date well back into the eighteenth century or even before. The earliest and most enduring of these was Sadler's Wells, north of the city; later, across the Thames in Surrey, an equestrian enterprise begun by Philip Astley in 1768 was followed by another, the Royal Circus, in 1782. Each of these structures had important connections with the development of London theatrical entertainment.

In the summer of 1683 some workmen discovered near Dick

---

[1] Mander and Mitchenson, *Lost Theatres*, pp. 485–491.
[2] Mander and Mitchenson, *Theatres of London*, p. 97.

Sadler's music house, north of the City near Islington, a well dating from a former age.[3] The waters proved to have medicinal properties like those at Tunbridge Wells, and a custom grew up of offering a combination of drink and entertainment at Sadler's Wells, as the establishment came to be called. Over the years the amusements expanded to include a variety of tight-rope walkers, dancers and other specialists. Singers such as the famous Mrs. Bland and John Braham made early appearances at the Wells. As the eighteenth century moved towards its close, more specifically theatrical fare developed. As early as 1753 Sadler's Wells had obtained a licence under the act of 1751 (25 George II) regulating places of public entertainment in London and Westminster and for twenty miles outside, and providing for mandatory licensing by local magistrates.[4] One of the specific targets of this law was Sadler's Wells itself, which had gained a reputation as a disorderly house. Fortunately for its proprietors, the Wells in the post-licensing period combined steady popularity with increasing respectability. A new, elegant theatre of brick built in 1765 opened a period of increasing attention paid to pantomime and musical theatrical entertainment. Around the close of the century the contributions, as writer and manager, of the younger Charles Dibdin, whose family's fortunes had become deeply involved with those of the London theatres, were still another sign that, by degrees, the entertainment available at the Islington spa was encroaching on patent house fare.

At the same time, the patent houses were emulating the methods of the Wells, not only in pantomime but in the interpolation of songs, dances and sometimes other special performances between the acts of plays, or even into the body of the drama itself. In fact the patent houses had been doing this on their own ever since the Restoration, but the increasing success of Sadler's Wells coincides with greater emphasis on extra-dramatic entertainment by Covent Garden and Drury

---

[3] Information on Sadler's Wells has been drawn from Baker; Dennis Arundell, *The Story of Sadler's Wells* (1965); and Mander and Mitchenson, *Theatres of London*.

[4] Arundell, *Sadler's Wells*, p. 18; Nicholson, pp. 125–126.

Lane. It is safe to say that, by 1800, these two theatres had provided their audiences with much the same variety of singing, dancing, rope-walking, tumbling, and pantomimic entertainments available at the Wells, although not nearly in so regular a fashion. The crucial difference was simply that the Sadler's Wells licence provided solely for these 'illegitimate' amusements; the regular drama, as always, was proscribed.

An excellent instance of the competition between the majors and the Wells occurred in 1789, occasioned by the English fascination with the fall of the Bastille. An entertainment entitled *The Bastille*, already in rehearsal at Covent Garden, was denied a licence by the Lord Chamberlain;[5] perhaps this sort of presentation by a patent theatre might have seemed to lend tacit official approval to the events depicted. Other theatres, however, were not so restricted. On 31 August, barely a month after the event itself, Sadler's Wells brought forth *Gallic Freedom; or, Vive La Liberté*, a spectacular recreation of the Bastille events.[6] An even earlier response came from the two transpontine houses. Astley's, known at this time as the Royal Grove, presented a version of the subject as early as 5 August,[7] and its close rival the Royal Circus did the same on that date.[8] Evidently, when practical business considerations were involved, the major houses were ready to throw in their lot with the minors. Despite the wording of the original patents and the subsequent laws enacted in their favour, the preservation of the legitimate drama sometimes ran a poor second to the prospect of large receipts.

The triumph of *Gallic Freedom* initiated at Sadler's Wells a custom of offering entertainments on topical themes that was

[5] *The Life and Times of Frederick Reynolds. Written by Himself* (1826), II, 54, cited by Nicoll, III, 19.

[6] Playbill for 1 September 1789 (Harvard Theatre Collection).

[7] Playbill (Harvard Theatre Collection).

[8] A. H. Saxon, *ThN*, 28 (1974), 133. Nicoll (III, 328) cites a performance of *Gallic Freedom* ten days earlier than the Wells', on 21 August, at the Royal Circus, but does not refer to the Wells' production. Nicoll also identifies an entertainment by John Dent called *The Bastille*, performed at the Royal Circus on 19 October, with the piece rehearsed at Covent Garden and then banned (III, 254; VI, 32). Saxon (pp. 133–5) provides further information on Dent.

to continue for some twenty-five years.[9] On what came to be called the Glorious First of June, 1794, Admiral Howe scored a victory against the French off Brittany. The event elicited instantaneous response from Britons generally and Sadler's Wells in particular. Only three days after the event, the Wells brought out a timely *Sons of Britannia, or, George for Old England*, whose general theme contrasted present-day French characteristics with traditional English virtues. Then the event itself was celebrated in late July with *Naval Triumph, or, The Tars of Old England*, whose spectacular effects included a display specifically in honour of 'that brave defender of his country's fame, Earl Howe'.[10] Sadler's Wells soon became known as the home of nautical drama, and its audience included a large proportion of sailors, who evidently liked the way the theatre idealized their lives. In a tribute to the Wells of his youth William Wordsworth recalled the emphasis there on nautical subjects and present-day events. Along with the 'Singers, Rope-dancers, Giants and Dwarfs, / Clowns, Conjurors, Posture-masters, Harlequins' that he saw, he remembered 'dramas of living Men' and events 'yet warm with life; a Sea-fight, / Shipwreck, or some domestic incident / The fame of which is scatter'd through the Land'.[11]

Given the Wells' reputation for nautical plays and its convenient situation opposite the New River, the brilliant innovation of its manager Charles Dibdin the younger in 1804 has the aura of the inevitable about it. The new season began in a theatre whose renovated stage featured a tank of real water in which naval battles were to be waged with scale model ships complete with firing cannon. Ships and crews alike were authentically detailed, and swimmers were hired to manipulate the craft through the filled tank, only three feet deep but ninety feet long. The piece that opened the theatre on 2 April 1804, entitled *The Siege of Gibraltar*, boasted some 117 ships. Not surprisingly, the profits of the 1804 season ran six times as

[9] Arundell, *Sadler's Wells*, p. 46.
[10] N.s., quoted by Arundell, *Sadler's Wells*, p. 53.
[11] *The Prelude*, ed. Ernest de Selincourt, 2nd edn. rev. by Helen Darbyshire (Oxford, 1959), 1805–6 text, VII, 293–294, 312–315.

great as before, a striking exception to generally prevailing losses.[12]

What gave the Wells its singularity is evident. What it shared with other London theatres is perhaps equally clear, for the encroachment of the minors on the hitherto exclusive territory of the patent houses was everywhere in evidence. By 1825, under the management of Charles Dibdin's younger brother Thomas, the Wells was able to open a ten-week season at Christmas in blithe disregard of the limits set by the 1787 licence, and with apparent impunity. From 1828, for a considerable period, the winter and summer seasons became virtually one.[13] Again, despite the licence, in a three-month period in 1830 the Wells paraded such workhorses of the legitimate repertoire as *The Merchant of Venice*, *Richard III*, *The Iron Chest*, *Pizarro*, *The Castle Spectre* and *Venice Preserv'd*.[14] There were nevertheless no recriminations from the patent houses, which by this time had been reduced to legal and, some thought, artistic impotence.

In the history of that decline the playhouses which grew up south of the Thames played their own essential part. The early life of these transpontine houses began with the birth of the modern circus in an amphitheatre erected by Philip Astley in the winter of 1778–79.[15] A former sergeant major in the Light Dragoons, Astley was an ardent enthusiast of horsemanship who for some ten years had been building an audience for displays of trick riding, but his performances were now expanding to include rope dancing, acrobatics, swordsmanship and feats of strength. The popularity of Astley's exhibitions was evidently high enough to induce his competitor Charles Hughes, proprietor of a riding school, to take Charles Dibdin the elder as partner and erect a rival structure. The Royal Circus and Philharmonic Academy, which welcomed its first audiences in 1782, was more than just another horse ring: it

[12] Arundell, *Sadler's Wells*, pp. 72, 74, 62.
[13] Arundell, *Sadler's Wells*, pp. 104, 108.
[14] Arundell, *Sadler's Wells*, p. 112.
[15] This account depends primarily on A. H. Saxon, *Enter Foot and Horse: A History of Hippodrama in England and France* (New Haven, 1968), pp. 10ff.

boasted a genuine stage. Dibdin's dream, he tells the readers of his memoirs, was to unite 'the business of the stage and the ring' by revivifying the ideals of ancient chivalry, representing spectacles on a stage and then ending with a joust, a tilting match, or some equally great event, 'so managed as to form a novel, and striking *coup-de-theatre*'.[16]

Dibdin's projected marriage of two arts did not occur, and the enterprise was ignominiously cut short by the Surrey magistrates, who ordered Hughes to close for operating without a licence. The ground had nevertheless been broken for a theatre in the proper sense of the term. By 1784 Astley was giving ballets and pantomimes on a stage of his own, and Hughes himself, having got rid of Dibdin, was back in business as well. Although Astley lost his first amphitheatre to fire in 1794 and his second likewise in 1803, his third, later under the impressive horseman Andrew Ducrow, survived until 1841. During the same years the Royal Circus led a less consistent existence. Under the management of James Jones and J. C. Cross its prosperity was interrupted by fire in 1805, and the poor returns on the subsequent building caused its lease to the ambitious and talented actor Robert William Elliston in 1809. Elliston, a man of the theatre entirely, made the riding ring into a pit and renamed his structure the Surrey Theatre, where he offered bills consisting of melodrama and the already almost ubiquitous burletta. A two-year reversion to a circus, from 1814 to 1816, was followed by the advent of Thomas Dibdin as lessee, his Sadler's Wells experience behind him but well in mind. From this point on, the Surrey remained permanently a theatre.

Although initially Elliston remained at the Surrey for only a few years, until 1814, he ended his career there also, serving as manager again from 1827 almost to the eve of his death in 1831.[17] Between these two periods he eventually became the lessee of Drury Lane for seven years beginning in 1819.[18] A

[16] *The Professional Life of Mr.* [Charles] *Dibdin, Written by Himself* (1803), II, 105.

[17] Baker, 392–394; see also George Raymond, *Memoirs of Robert William Elliston* (1846, repr. New York, 1969), II, 528–533.   [18] *Survey of London*, p. 23.

figure of great importance to the theatre of his age, Elliston found himself alternately on one side, then the other, of the incessant battle over patent rights and their alleged violation, and in the case of the controversial definition of burletta his voice would be, as always, clearly heard.

By 1800, then, the theatrical situation in London was already complex and moving unmistakably in the direction of ever greater competitiveness. In addition to Covent Garden, Drury Lane and the summer Haymarket, as well as the King's opera house, some seven theatres in and around London proper were offering, at least intermittently and for the most part regularly, entertainment of a pronounced theatrical nature: Sadler's Wells, Astley's, the Royal Circus, the Royalty in east London, Dibdin's Sans Souci, the King's, Pantheon and the first Lyceum. This last structure, built in 1771–2 and converted to a small theatre in 1794 by Samuel Arnold, failed to obtain a licence, but by 1799 various entertainments were being presented. It was here that the famous wax works of Madame Tussaud first enthralled Londoners in 1802.[19] Amazingly, despite the series of fires that gutted the theatres of this time, and of times to follow, and so determined their history to a great extent, not a single one of the playhouses in question became a permanent casualty.

In addition to the 1809 Covent Garden and the 1812 Drury Lane, other new theatres were constructed during the first two decades of the century. Even when continued rebuilding (and renaming) is considered, no pattern should be discerned in this fact other than that of free commercial enterprise. Still, the result with respect to London playgoing was an ever greater variety of opportunity. The significance was not lost on the managers and shareholders of the major houses, who hoped, so often in vain, for a decent return on investment, to say nothing of old-fashioned profits.

The first two of these nineteenth-century structures, the Olympic Pavilion and the Sans Pareil, appeared in the same year, 1806.

Using the timbers from an old dismantled warship, Philip

[19] Mander and Mitchenson, *Theatres of London*, p. 273.

Astley built a tent-like theatre in Wych Street, between Drury Lane and the City.[20] The Olympic Pavilion, as he called it, intended to duplicate the success of his summer amphitheatre with a winter house, disappointed his expectations despite the lively existence it led from its opening in September 1806. Astley's interior offered the conjunction of stage and ring familiar to transpontine audiences, and the speciality of the house still consisted of a combination of equestrian spectacle with staged ballet and pantomime. A writer in the *Monthly Mirror* describes the seating plan as one emphasizing both the arena itself and a large pit, with a gallery directly behind and a small box area above, the whole comprising a house of only £80.[21] On the basis of this arrangement one may speculate that Astley hoped to attract audiences generally similar to those at his Surrey amphitheatre but perhaps, in the process, to draw upon the greater range of spectators found at the major houses nearby. Whatever gains may have materialized, success as a whole eluded him, for reasons that remain unclear. Modifications in the variety of the bill and even repeated changes of name—Pavilion Theatre (1809), Olympic Saloon, Astley's Middlesex Amphitheatre, Astley's Theatre (1810), New Pavilion Theatre (1811), Theatre Royal Pavilion (Astley's) (1812)—were of no avail. Now an old man, Astley sold out early in 1813 and died the following year.

The purchaser was none other than the redoubtable Robert William Elliston, whose innate self-confidence and experience at the Surrey had evidently fired a desire to snatch success where others had failed. Emblematic of his aggressive instincts was the name he bestowed on his remodelled investment: Little Drury Lane Theatre. Undaunted by the closure soon forced on him by the Lord Chamberlain at the instigation of the Drury Lane management, who for some reason felt themselves infringed upon, Elliston obtained a new burletta licence and capitulated, to a degree, by changing the name of his theatre to the Olympic. Reopening late in 1813, he

[20] Mander and Mitchenson, *Lost Theatres*, pp. 243ff.
[21] September 1806, quoted in Mander and Mitchenson, *Lost Theatres*, p.

followed a precedent established by the Sans Pareil, in the Strand not far away, by offering a weekly run of a single bill. Apparently the first week was comprised of 'a Divertisement by Miss Green and her Pupils', an occasional address by Miss Dow, a 'Grand Melo-Drama' entitled *Blood Will Have Blood*, and a 'favourite Interlude' called *The Christmas Holydays, or School's Up*[22]—all of this, it should be observed, well within the lines of his licence.

Under Elliston the Olympic prospered. Spurred by success, in 1818 he put some £2,500 into a partial rebuilding project, and his theatre, known for a while as the New Olympic, created a more fashionable audience and even more attractive profits. By this time Elliston was evidently primed for greater exploits. Fortified by undying aspirations and a healthy bank account,[23] he took a lease on the Theatre Royal, Drury Lane. Gradually, but inevitably, his fortunes began to wane. After letting the Olympic to a series of mismanagers, Elliston finally found a buyer in the person of a businessman named John Scott, the former owner of the Sans Pareil. The paltry sum he realized, however, could not rescue 'the Great Lessee', as he was somewhat ironically known, from the bankruptcy he had unexpectedly fallen heir to, utterly broken on the cruel rack of major theatre management, in 1826.

A decade of melodrama at the Olympic under Scott at length gave way to one of the most significant managements of the nineteenth century. Beginning in 1831, the fascinating dancer Eliza Vestris turned manager and made the Olympic the home of tasteful, well-rehearsed burletta, reclaiming some of this theatre's lost audiences and, together with the dramatist J. R. Planché, setting high standards and introducing important innovations in production. This, the third and last structure on the site of the original Olympic, remained until as late as 1905, finishing a century of history.

In the same year of the Olympic's birth, 1806, John Scott, having realized large sums from the success of a new washing

[22] *The Times* advertisement, 1 January 1814, quoted in Mander and Mitchenson, *Lost Theatres*, pp. 261–262.
[23] Raymond, *Memoirs of Elliston*, II, 198–201.

product called True Blue, built in the Strand an appropriate showcase for his daughter's considerable talents (Plate 4).[24] The entertainments at the Sans Pareil Theatre quickly justified Scott's partiality to his daughter's ambitions. One of the earliest surviving playbills, dating from the pre-Easter period of 1807, announces a programme whose variety and novelty must have had genuine appeal:

The New Theatre, SANS PAREIL, STRAND, Opposite the ADELPHI, This and every Evening during Lent, WEDNESDAYS *and* FRIDAYS *excepted*, Will be Performed the following ENTERTAINMENTS: PART I. A New Musical Piece, with Recitation in Two Parts, called RURAL VISITORS, or SINGULARITY: The whole Written, Selected, Composed, and will be Spoken, Sung, and Accompanied, by MISS SCOTT. PART II. A THUNDER STORM, PART III. An entire New and interesting SPECTACLE, representing apparently in the Air, AN ANCIENT GRAND BATTLE IN SHADOW, In which several Thousand Figures, armed in the Costume of their Time, are seen engaged, as said by GODFREY of BOUILLON to have appeared to him while he led the Christian Army under the Walls of JERUSALEM. *To conclude with an Elegant New Constructed* ARTIFICIAL FIRE WORK, In a TEMPLE Superbly Illuminated. THE WHOLE ACCOMPANIED WITH APPROPRIATE MUSIC.[25]

In the detailed description of the theatre printed at the bottom of the bill, a fact of moot significance stands out. The seating area was comprised solely 'of a capacious Pit and a Range of Fifteen Boxes . . . and Four Other Boxes on the Stage.—There is no Gallery.' Little is known of the composition of the Sans Pareil audience, but it seems likely that the emphasis on a 'capacious' pit invites a homogeneous audience, perhaps (as in the case of the Olympic) representing a notably smaller social range than the major theatres, but aiming, at the same time, at a more fashionable, moneyed class which might be attracted by the exclusiveness suggested by stage boxes. Whatever the

[24] This account is based on information drawn from Edward Wedlake Brayley, *Historical and Descriptive Accounts of the Theatres of London* (1826 [for 1827]); Baker; and Mander and Mitchenson, *Theatres of London*.
[25] Playbill (Harvard Theatre Collection). Nicoll dates the first performance of *Rural Visitors* as 16 January 1807—IV, 530.

intention, the experimental omission of the gallery was at length repaired, for by January 1810 the prices of admission indicated in the bills included a one-shilling gallery.[26]

A typical evening's entertainment, much of it written, composed and performed by the indefatigable Miss Scott, comprised three and often four pieces: pantomimes; dances, interludes, and other special attractions of a spectacular nature; and pieces essentially dramatic, consistently designated as burletta and often further identified as melodrama or farce.[27] The bill for 22 January 1810, for example, featured an 'Interlude' called *Lilliput Island, or, Automaton Shadows*; a 'Musical Melo Dramatic Burletta' entitled *The Bashaw*; *Or Adventures of Three Spaniards*; and a 'Comic Pantomime', *Necromancer or, The Golden Key*—the latter two by Miss Scott, who also played the Bashaw. As the decade progressed, these entertainments apparently became more highly developed. *The Intrigue; or, Love's Failure*, given 25 June 1810, is called simply a 'Melo Dramatic Burletta', but *Whakham and Windham* of 8 March 1814 is styled a 'Broad Farcical Comick Burletta', and *The Inscription; or, Indian Hunters* of the same date is described as a 'Melo-Dramatic Romance, or Naval Burletta' (Sidney Nelson, a Midshipman, by Miss Scott).

Miss Scott's name remained before the London theatregoing public—she was apparently the Miss Scott who played the title role in the Surrey's great nautical success *Black Ey'd Susan* in 1829—but by 1819 her father had sold the Sans Pareil to Messrs. Jones and Rodwell, who renamed the theatre the Adelphi. The price paid, £25,000, suggests that the high reputation of the Adelphi in the 1820s and 1830s was built on an estimable foundation. During several changes of management in these years the theatre developed the specialities that made the phrase 'Adelphi drama' one of instant recognition. The staple fare was melodrama, which came to be intermingled with dramatizations of the novels of Walter Scott. Then, in 1821, a spectacular success occurred with the staging of William Moncrieff's *Tom and Jerry; or, Life in London*, adapted from the

26 Playbill for 22 January 1810 (Folger Shakespeare Library).

27 Sans Pareil playbills, 1810–19 (Folger Shakespeare Library).

hugely popular novel of sporting life by Pierce Egan and featuring accurate representations of real-life scenes and characters. Although the play almost failed the first night,[28] such was its eventual popularity that it set a record of 100 consecutive performances, from 26 November 1821 to 30 March 1822.[29]

Even this record was surpassed several years later, under the management of two former major-theatre actors, Frederick Yates and Daniel Terry, the latter backed partly by his friend Walter Scott. Edward Fitzball's dramatization of Fenimore Cooper's sea novel *The Pilot* had deftly altered characters and sympathies to accord with British patriotic sentiment. Assisted by the acting of T. P. Cooke as Long Tom Coffin, the play drew enthusiastic audiences for some 200 nights, beginning on 31 October 1825.[30] As in the instance of *Tom and Jerry*, a sense of real authenticity prevailed in the production, for Cooke had actually served in the Royal Navy before making his debut at the Royalty in 1804 and was at the height of his fame as a portrayer of convincing, heart-stirring nautical characters.[31] Despite inevitable financial uncertainties (both Terry and his successor Charles Mathews, the famous one-man entertainer, lost money) the Adelphi sustained its enviable reputation into the 1830s with plays that included dramatic versions of novels of Charles Dickens. In the year of Mathews' death, 1834, the Adelphi was known as 'by far the most fashionably attended theatre in London',[32] a judgement made at the obvious expense of Covent Garden and Drury Lane.

Meanwhile, in 1810, another theatre had opened, somewhat to the north of the patent theatres and outside the district of Westminster. As far back as 1772 concert rooms existed on a site in Tottenham Street, later patronized by King George III. The chequered history of the structure in the early nineteenth century, used for private theatricals and then for a circus, was

[28] Baker, p. 417.
[29] Mander and Mitchenson, *Theatres of London*, p. 16.
[30] Mander and Mitchenson, *Theatres of London*, p. 16.
[31] Baker, p. 421.
[32] Mander and Mitchenson, *Theatres of London*, p. 17.

not altered for the better when J. Paul, a gunsmith whose wife entertained theatrical ambitions, fitted up the premises for stage performances. The New Theatre in Tottenham Street, alternately known as the Tottenham Theatre,[33] became a costly failure. Varying managements and fortunes and changing names mark the devious course of this theatre through the sketchy annals of its subsequent history. It was not until much later in the century that Marie Wilton took over what had come to be known as 'The Dusthole', transformed it into the Prince of Wales's Royal Theatre, and provided the young T. W. Robertson with an audience that witnessed a significant renewal of the vigour of English drama.

Only one other theatre appeared during the second decade of this century. Under the patronage of the Prince of Saxe Coburg and Princess Charlotte, whose intercession had been instrumental in obtaining a licence,[34] the Royal Coburg Theatre arose in Lambeth, across Waterloo Bridge, in 1818. The licence was, of course, strictly for the ill-defined form of burletta, and the Coburg became known as a place for melodrama, often lurid pieces connected with some topical subject. The opening play, for example, written by the actor and Coburg producer William Barrymore and called *Trial by Battle; or, Heaven defend the Right*, concerned the murder of Mary Ashford, whose alleged assailant had been tried only a short time before the theatre opened.[35] The accused man, Abraham Thornton, appealed to an old statute allowing trial by battle against his accuser, Mary Ashford's brother. The gauntlet Thornton threw down was not taken up, he was discharged, and the case remained unsolved. The dramatic treatment of this subject was presumably typical of the extreme style that made the Coburg 'the very haunt and refuge of the melodramatic muse', according to a contemporary writer. At

[33] Mander and Mitchenson, *Theatres of London*, p. 181. See also Richard L. Lorenzen, 'Managers of the Old Prince of Wales's Theatre', *Theatre Notebook*, 24 (1969), 32–36; and Lorenzen, 'The Old Prince of Wales's Theatre', *Theatre Notebook*, 25 (1971), 132–145.

[34] Mander and Mitchenson, *Theatres of London*, pp. 238–239.

[35] See the account in Baker, p. 397.

this theatre, he explained, '"murder bares her red arm" with most appalling vividness; there the genius of robbery reigns triumphant on his festive throne; there the sheeted ghosts do squeak and gibber across the frighted stage, and all the sublimities of horror are to be found there, in their most high and palmy state'.[36] The reputation of the Coburg for fare of this sort appears to account for its popularity with the residents of Lambeth. At the same time, the theatre held a general reputation for the splendour of its architecture and interior. Perhaps this increased its attractiveness to audiences on either side of the river, but the truth is that far too little is known about the audiences of many theatres in this age, and generalizations must remain tentative.

From the founding of the Coburg in 1818, the building of theatres in London came to a virtual standstill for a considerable time. The Haymarket, whose history is not typical of the period, was rebuilt in 1821, but this is quite a rare exception in the decade, so far as London proper is concerned. In the 1820s and 1830s theatres sprang up in the outlying districts—the New Sussex and the Clarence to the north, the Bower Saloon in the south—and in the east of London the New Pavilion appeared in Whitechapel by 1826, followed by the Garrick (1830), the City of London (1835) in Bishopsgate, the Royal Standard in Shoreditch by 1836, and others. A full list must await a complete stage calendar for the period. These were theatres serving a predominantly local clientele, just the sort of audience that John Palmer's Royalty sought to benefit back in 1787. The growth of these suburban theatres in the 1830s implies the inability of patent theatre proprietors to prevent them from opening their doors. The almost total absence of new theatres in the decade before, however, can be taken as a sign of the financial difficulties encountered by major and minor theatres alike. Moreover, the important question of money was complicated by other problems even less easy to describe. In attempting to carry on the grand tradition of the eighteenth-century theatre, providing something like total variety for an entire metropolitan audience,

[36] N.s., quoted by Baker, p. 397.

the managements of Covent Garden and Drury Lane had been confronted with the rude fact that a new age may arbitrarily reject the values of the old. Accommodation, even if it ruins integrity, was the newly evident price of survival.

It was a lesson the minor theatres had learned long before. An account of the growth of London theatres in this age remains incomplete without discussion of the one dramatic form whose repeated use epitomizes the struggle of the minors for survival. That form is not melodrama but *burletta*, which from a legal point of view included not only melodrama but a fair host of other phenomena more difficult to define. Despite the obscurity of the term itself, the issue of burletta was of fundamental importance in the age of Kean, not because it had some mysterious claim to generic sovereignty over more classical forms, but because the minor theatres were blatantly using it as a legal umbrella to cover whatever theatrical pieces, 'legitimate' or otherwise, they had a mind to perform. And in doing so, it was alleged, they were ruining the patent theatres, the patent theatre proprietors, and the national drama in the process.

The history of burletta is closely connected with the development of the minor theatres of London in the late eighteenth and early nineteenth centuries. 'When I was a boy,' Charles Kemble recalled in 1832, reminiscing about the happy days before he became proprietor of a patent theatre, 'they used at Sadler's Wells and Astley's, and Hughes's, which is now the Surrey, to give a certain entertainment which they designated burlettas, and these entertainments . . . were written in a sort of doggrel [*sic*] verse, and were accompanied by a piano-forte, the person playing in the orchestra; it was, in short, a recitative, accompanied by instruments in the orchestra.'[37] Kemble's reasonably accurate description of the form was nevertheless only a relic of the past. By 1832 the position of anyone with a vested interest in Covent Garden or Drury Lane was the bitter opposite of enviable, owing in great measure to the impossibility of defining burletta in

[37] *Report*, Q. 735.

a court of law. For what could not be defined could not be prohibited.

The practice of employing burletta to evade the strict letter of the law had been slow in developing. In the middle of the previous century a new form of comic opera had been introduced at the King's Opera House in the Haymarket. Called *burletta* by its Italian practitioners, it offered a variety of intermezzo-like entertainment as a joking contrast to serious opera, but its form, a combination of recitative and song, was the same as its ponderous counterpart.[38] The popularity of the novelty can be seen in mid-century records of opera house performances and in the almost immediate anglicization for summer audiences at Marylebone Gardens. Yet the novelty was not by any means total. As early as 1737 Henry Fielding had brought out at his little theatre in the Haymarket a burlesque of Italian opera by Henry Carey entitled *The Dragon of Wantley*. Carey's piece was a delightful and pointed combination of the mock-heroic with tuneful music, but its most distinguishing feature, viewed from the standpoint of subsequent theatrical history, was its total lack of spoken dialogue. Like Italian serious opera and its later *burletta* counterpart, *The Dragon of Wantley* was composed entirely of airs and recitative. The Italian operatic *burletta* had evidently touched a certain spirit indigenous to English life and art.

From the beginning, then, the technical form of burletta was clear, almost rigorous; but its practitioners employed it in an invincible spirit of freedom. When Italian burletta players were imported to Dublin in the early 1760s, a resident wit named Kane O'Hara burlesqued them in turn with a piece called *Midas*, subtitled *An English Burletta* and composed completely of recitative and song. The transfer of *Midas* to Covent Garden, after a season of Italian burletta there in the previous decade, fixed the permanent attention of legitimate theatre audiences on the form. The most important single fact about the early history of burletta is its introduction into the major theatre repertory, for the early presence of burletta there was itself the

[38] Charles Burney, *A General History of Music*, ed. Frank Mercer (1935, repr. New York, 1957), II, 599.

precedent for its attempted adoption, with increasing success, by minor theatres. Initially burletta had no taint of the illegitimate about it. The patent theatres had as unquestioned a right to it as they did to ballad opera, Shakespearean comedy or any other native or naturalized English theatrical product. The crucial point is simply the patent theatres' perennial insistence on their monopoly on the spoken word, whatever else they might wish to perform. Spoken dialogue was the hallmark of legitimacy.

For the minor theatres of the late eighteenth century, then, the existence of burletta—the one verbal form found at the major houses which contained no spoken dialogue—proved a unique opportunity to present pieces essentially dramatic. Early minor houses like Sadler's Wells and Astley's had originally been places of exclusively non-dramatic entertainment, but by the Acts of 1751 and 1755 local magistrates were allowed to authorize certain 'publick entertainment' in order to regulate it.[39] Seizing on the vagueness of the phrase, these places of amusement began to enlarge the scope of their offerings. By 1787 Astley's had been able to have burletta explicitly included in an amphitheatre licence that already permitted equestrian entertainments.[40] By 1807 the practice of presenting burletta was common enough for John Scott, the proprietor of the new Sans Pareil, to petition the Lord Chamberlain to add burletta to his licence in order to make it conform to his actual practice.[41]

Towards the second decade of the nineteenth century several innovations occurred which speeded the progress of burletta towards the state of legitimate drama. At the Royal Circus, newly leased by Elliston in 1809, burletta began to be used to transform legitimate plays into presentations consistent with its still wholly musical form of airs and 'doggrel' verse sung in recitative. Elliston's own first appearance at his new theatre was

[39] Dewey Ganzel, 'Patent Wrongs and Patent Theatres', *PMLA*, 76 (1961), 386–387.

[40] Nicholson, p. 283.

[41] Historical MSS. Commission, Report XIII[4], p. 505, quoted in Nicholson, pp. 283–284.

as Macheath in a 'Burletta melodram' version of *The Beggar's Opera*. In the same season he transmogrified *Macbeth* into a ballet of action, with music, and subsequently went on to play burletta versions of such traditional patent theatre favourites as *The Beaux' Stratagem* and *A Bold Stroke for a Wife*.[42] The practice of Miss Scott at the Sans Pareil of rifling the works of French dramatists, which she 'rendered Burletta',[43] suggests the possibilities open to managers with sufficient enterprise and daring. Nor was this the only advance in the ability of the minor theatres to infringe on the rights of the major houses. Around this same time Charles Dibdin the younger, manager of Sadler's Wells since 1800, 'dismissed the Piano from the Orchestra', according to his own account, 'and introduced dialogue, spoken in prose only'....[44]

Significantly, no record has emerged of Dibdin's being prosecuted for this flagrant illegality, for in an earlier day John Palmer was sent to prison and recorded as a 'rogue and vagrant' for speaking prose in a performance at the Royal Circus in 1789.[45] Moreover, it is evident from Dibdin's account that performance of burletta at Sadler's Wells at this period was already characterized to some extent by the spoken word, even before the dismissal of piano accompaniment from the orchestra. Writing at about the same time as Dibdin, in 1830, the former comic dramatist and present official examiner of plays George Colman the younger summed up the process by which the burletta he insisted should be 'entirely musical' became indistinguishable from the regular drama. After performing burletta for some time strictly according to definition, he explained, the minor theatres 'made their Recitative appear like Prose, by the actor running one line into another, and slurring over the rhyme;—soon after, a harpsichord was touch'd *now and then*, as an accompaniment to the actor;—sometimes once in a minute;—then once in five minutes;—

[42] Raymond, *Memoirs of Elliston*, I, 403–404, II, 3.
[43] Playbill, 8 March 1810 (Folger Shakespeare Library).
[44] *Professional & Literary Memoirs of Charles Dibdin the Younger*, ed. George Speaight (1956), pp. 111–112.
[45] Jacob Decastro, *The Memoirs of J. Decastro, Comedian* (1824), pp. 122–125.

at last—not at all;—till, in the process of time, musical and rhyming dialogue has been abandoned'. . . .[46] The virtually unlimited licence enjoyed by the minor theatres by the end of the third decade of the century was a far cry from conditions prevailing twenty or thirty years before. W. T. Moncrieff, the prolific author of the famous 'extravaganza' of 1821, *Tom and Jerry; or, Life in London* (billed, of course, as a burletta), indicated the extent of the progress in describing the sort of burletta liable to be found at the minors around 1800 or 1810. Those 'inexplicable pieces of dumb shew', he observed with punning intent, were

unutterable morceaux, which went under the name of Spectacles, and of which the BLACK CASTLE, and BLOOD-RED KNIGHT were memorable specimens; all that could not be rendered clear by action, was told by means of what were called 'scrolls': pieces of linen, on which whatever the Dramatis Personae wished to communicate to each other, for the better understanding of the audience, was expressed in writing, painted on the cloth, and which the Performers alternately fetched from the different sides of the stage, and presented to the full view of the public. . . .[47]

In the course of the half-century up to 1832, when the newly elected M.P. Edward Lytton Bulwer chaired a parliamentary inquiry into the causes of the decline of the drama, the apparently harmless musical entertainment of burletta had been turned into a sharp, efficacious wedge driven between the closed portals of the legitimate drama. The lucid simplicity of its original non-spoken form made it a safe refuge, even as the course of theatrical history was changing its actual shape virtually out of recognition.

The encroachments of the minor theatres, however, were only the foremost of numerous difficulties faced by the major houses. The years following the transformation, in the 1790s, of Covent Garden and Drury Lane into unprecedentedly large structures were marked by an increasing tendency to forsake

[46] Colman, I, 52–53.

[47] Moncrieff, 'Remarks' on *Tom and Jerry*, 2nd edn. (Thomas Richardson, n.d.), p. v.

the demands of speech for the pleasures of the eye. Older, more 'natural' acting styles had to capitulate to the conditions of enlarged auditoriums and deepened stages. Because of the great attractiveness of musical production, the theatres had been for some time at the expense of keeping a large company of both actors and singers. Moreover, the nature of the repertoire was beginning to change, under pressure from the success of burletta, pantomime and the general variety at the minor theatres, and from the insistent demands of an audience whose apparent preference was, as the younger Colman lamented, for 'pageantry and shew'. There is no use in talking if people cannot hear, Colman tartly observed in a song delivered at his Haymarket in 1795:

> Let your Shakespeares and Jonsons go hang, go hang!
> Let your Otways and Drydens go drown!
> Give us but Elephants and white Bulls enough,
> And we'll take in all the town.[48]

Spectacle was of course much more expensive to produce than the regular drama. The two major theatres nevertheless continued to earn profits, if not spectacular ones, and their managers continued to think of them as the home—the refuge, in fact—of legitimate drama. No matter that the times had contrived to make them an orphanage for other forms as well. Over the years following his debut as Hamlet at Drury Lane in 1783, John Philip Kemble had built a considerable reputation playing Shakespearean and other English classical heroes. His austere acting style, antiquarian interests, and financial resources made him uniquely well equipped to purchase a one-sixth share in Covent Garden and to take over as actor-manager, which he did in 1803, having quarrelled with Sheridan.[49] Kemble had every right to expect a considerable return on an investment he undoubtedly considered both monetary and cultural, and meanwhile he proceeded in mounting a series of Shakespearean productions notable for

[48] Closing song in *New Hay at the Old Market* (1795).

[49] Herschel Baker, *John Philip Kemble: The Actor in His Theatre* (Cambridge, Mass., 1942), p. 274.

their combination of atmospheric historical settings and extensive pageantry with the peerless classic acting of his sister Mrs. Siddons and himself.

He surely could not have anticipated the double calamity that lay in store for him.

The difficulties began when Covent Garden burned to the ground in September 1808. With unexampled swiftness a new structure was planned, financed, built, and scheduled to open on 18 September 1809. A week before, the management announced that because of the large amount expended in rebuilding the theatre the prices of admission unavoidably must be raised, in the cases of box and pit, from 6s. to 7s. and from 3s. 6d. to 4s. Neither Kemble nor the rest of the management paid any attention to stirrings of discontent at the news, and Robert Smirke's Greek Revival masterpiece opened its doors to an apparently eager and very full crowd of spectators. All went well through the initial singing of the anthem, but when Kemble, arrayed in a new, expensive costume for Macbeth, stepped forward to deliver a preliminary address, there was a sudden, deafening uproar. Kemble's speech went unheard amidst 'vollies of hissing, hooting, groans, and cat-calls' and intermittently audible cries of 'No imposition', 'No Catalani', and 'Old Prices' (Plate 5).[50]

Riots had for years formed an occasional part of the adventure of London playgoing, but in this case the degree of unanimity and the fury of its sustenance for some three months were unprecedented. The most immediate cause, ostensibly, was the rise in the cost of admission, and the revolt immediately became known as the O.P. ('Old Prices') Riot. But, as Leigh Hunt and others remarked, true theatre lovers would be unlikely to make such a large fuss over sixpence or a shilling by themselves.[51]

Prices aside, the most specific grievance was the engagement of the famous Italian singer Angelica Catalani at an exorbitant sum, an arrangement galling to insular mentalities. More

[50] *Covent Garden Journal*, ed. J. J. Stockdale (1810), I, 149–150.

[51] *Examiner*, 19 November 1809, in *Leigh Hunt's Dramatic Criticism 1808–1831*, ed. L. H. and C. W. Houtchens (New York, 1949), p. 33.

important, and more infuriating, was the increase in the number of private boxes, rented by the season, and a corresponding decrease in gallery seating. As early as 1792, when the old theatre was refurbished, the second, one-shilling gallery had been eliminated and then, after riotous protest, restored. Again in 1803 the 'slips' (side continuations of the two-shilling gallery) were made into boxes and the frontispiece was raised in order to allow installation of sixteen private boxes. The new theatre, however, had three whole tiers of boxes, the third exclusively private.[52] Leigh Hunt, whose sensibilities were in many respects representative of the outraged audiences', commented that taking a whole tier from the 'lovers of the Theatre' in order 'to make privacies for the luxurious great' was an offence to national habits.[53] Evidently this exclusiveness was the most disturbing factor. James Boaden, friend and biographer of Kemble and Mrs. Siddons, acknowledged the point, but took another view of it in explaining that the idea was to compete with the attractiveness of seating at the Italian Opera and thereby to woo its audiences to Covent Garden:

By devoting one entire tier to the nobility and gentry, the proprietors of Covent Garden Theatre could offer to their patrons a box, accessible at any time, with an anti-room, when they chose to withdraw for conversation or refreshments; there was, besides, a general saloon, for the occasional promenade of the privileged orders, and every arrangement made to render a public place of entertainment to *them* as select and private as their own residences— they quitted their boxes by exclusive staircases, and left the theatre from doors equally devoted to themselves.[54]

Elsewhere, Boaden admitted that the real objection of the rioters was to the 'absolute seclusion of a *privileged order* from all *vulgar contact*'.[55]

Taken in this context, the vague cries of 'No imposition' shouted at Kemble when the rioting began may well have

[52] *Survey of London*, pp. 35, 93, 96.
[53] *Examiner*, 19 November 1809, in *Hunt's Dramatic Criticism*, p. 33.
[54] James Boaden, *Memoirs of Mrs. Siddons* (1827), II, 369–370.
[55] James Boaden, *Memoirs of the Life of John Philip Kemble* (1825), II, 492.

referred to the forcing of anti-democratic distinctions on a British public audience. There were also suggestions that the intimacy of the anterooms would encourage debauchery, for which London theatres already had a considerable well-earned reputation. In any case, what was interpreted as the high-handed treatment of the audience by a small group of egregious profiteers touched a depth of responsiveness previously unknown to major theatre managers and proprietors. From the opening on 18 September the riots continued unabated for sixty-seven nights, until finally the Covent Garden proprietorship capitulated and order was restored on 15 December.[56] During this three-month period it was virtually futile to go to the theatre for the purpose of attending to the play, so loud and distracting were the continual interruptions of the organizers of the riot and their followers. An attempt to cool things off by closing the theatre while a disinterested committee adjudicated the theatre's claims of imminent financial ruin failed when the committee's report, supporting the proprietors, was rejected out of hand by the rioters. Finally, on 14 December, a large party of them dined at the Crown and Anchor Tavern for the purpose of accepting conciliation from Kemble, spokesman for the now desperate management. At this 'O.P. Banquet' the terms proposed were that the private boxes were to be reduced to the scale prevailing in 1802; admission prices for the pit were to revert to the former 3s. 6d., the boxes remaining at 7s.; in addition, an apology would be made to the public, an offensive box-keeper dismissed, and all legal proceedings against the rioters discontinued.[57] The terms were immediately accepted.

The riots finally over, Kemble and his colleagues settled down once more to the business of public entertainment, welcomed again by an audience now in the mood for less strenuous pleasures but always ready to exert what the banqueters toasted as 'the antient and indisputable right of the pit'.[58] The damage, however, had been done, and lastingly. The O.P. Riots had raised an issue of great symbolic value

[56] *Covent Garden Journal*, I, 139, 289.

[57] *Covent Garden Journal*, I, 136–137. [58] *Covent Garden Journal*, I, 126.

deeply felt in the charged atmosphere of this pre-Reform era. No doubt it hastened the retreat from the audience of many of the very persons the proprietors had hoped to hold, and confirmed in others their prior decision to abandon the public theatre altogether. At the same time a period of financial troubles had been ushered in, owing to a number of complex causes but precipitated by the continuing reluctance of the major theatres to face the facts of a changing age and audience.

The financial records that survive for Covent Garden and Drury Lane are fairly full but at times ambiguous; patterns are difficult to discern. For example, according to one set of figures the overall average of nightly receipts at Drury Lane for the six seasons from 1803–4 until the burning of the theatre in 1808–9 is £261. The average for the first six seasons in the new theatre, from 1812–13 to 1817–18, is exactly the same.[59] The receipts for the first of these later seasons (1812–13), however, averaged a nearly miraculous £370. Without this distorting figure, the average for the later years falls to £239.

These amounts by themselves do not, of course, tell the whole story. Immediately behind the financial plight of both Covent Garden and Drury Lane in the post-conflagration period lies the dreary arithmetic of colossal, insufficiently funded debt, partly the result of inadequate insurance on the previous structures. The situation was also a product of the much higher overhead resulting from war-inflated prices and the need to maintain constant staffs of hundreds of persons in the theatres. In 1832 Captain John Forbes, then a proprietor of Covent Garden, testified that 'some 1,000 persons' were constantly employed at his theatre and an unknown number of others directly or indirectly engaged.[60] Weekly pay remunerated numerous actors, actresses, singers, dancers, and other specialists who, because of the great variety attempted by the managers, appeared with relative infrequency. And all of these difficulties were aggravated by the inroads made by the

---

[59] Rounded to the nearest whole pound; see the report of the Drury Lane sub-committee printed in an anonymous pamphlet, *An Authentic Statement of Facts* (1818), p. 85.

[60] *Report*, Qq. 1994–95.

growing minor houses on the audiences of legitimate theatre. Analysis of a typical season in the second decade would show a repertory having much in common with that of twenty years before, but comparison of corresponding tables of nightly receipts would reveal that the legitimate drama was no longer able to hold its own. According to the Covent Garden proprietor Harris, from the rebuilding of that theatre in 1809 up to 1821 not a shilling was cleared from the regular drama. It was the profit made on the annual Christmas pantomime that offset other losses and enabled the theatre to realize a net gain.[61]

There were exceptions to the dismal general rule, to be sure. Shakespeare still had the capacity to attract, if produced with an eye like Kemble's for spectacular amplification of the text. The most important exception, aside from the perennially popular pantomime, was the appearance of an actor or actress who, in the language of siege and conquest, could take the town by storm. In the season of 1804–5 a child prodigy named William Henry Betty, quickly dubbed the Young Roscius, virtually eclipsed all other interests with his short-lived brilliance. Ten years later there appeared another, more mature actor whose unorthodox assault on jaded audiences held out hope of lasting triumph. When Edmund Kean made his Drury Lane debut as Shylock in the winter of 1813–14, his emergence was greeted almost immediately with critical acclaim unheard for a generation. To the proprietors of the theatre, however, it was the popular clamour for formerly vacant seats that spoke in more eloquent tones. That Kean seemed to have invented a wholly new style of Shakespearean acting was presumably of lesser concern. That he might, in the process, infuse new blood into a financially anaemic theatre was a more vital consideration. For if that theatre should otherwise succumb to its killing debts, it would make no difference whether Kean was a brash, importunate interloper in borrowed robes or the true heir to a great and still living tradition.

[61] Abstract of Harris's deposition in Chancery, summarized by Francis Place in *Report*, Qq. 3706–7.

CHAPTER FOUR

Acting and the Repertory Theatre

A century after Edmund Kean made his Drury Lane debut on 26 January 1814 historians were still perpetuating the almost mythical quality of his arrival. This 'obscure country tragedian', said one latter-day writer, 'had been engaged in sheer desperation, and brought up from Exeter, a very model of a strolling player, shabby, almost shoeless, whom the mediocrities treated at rehearsal with unconcealed contempt'. . . . Kean, however, scored a 'resounding' success, the story continues, and by the next morning 'all London was ringing with the fame of the new actor'.[1]

Myths tell important truths, and in the case of Kean the truth is that, poor and inelegant as he was, he possessed a wayward genius that seized the imaginations of playgoers. That he rescued Drury Lane from the brink of financial disaster is a truth, too, but a much less simple one. Inside of two months his contract had been renegotiated and his weekly salary raised to £20. The managing committee headed by the wealthy brewer Samuel Whitbread had given Kean several cash presents, sure signs of future profits already counted.[2] The fact is, however, that even Kean's great drawing power did not have a lasting effect. Drury Lane was so deeply in debt, holding obligations to shareholders in both the present theatre of

[1] Baker, pp. 88–89.
[2] H. N. Hillebrand, *Edmund Kean* (New York, 1933), p. 120.

1809–12 and Sheridan's burned-down playhouse of 1794, that even Whitbread himself despaired. Following the formation, over his objections, of a new committee in June 1815, he committed suicide.[3]

Yet, all the while, Kean continued to rise on the quick tide of his fortunes, as if the continuing crises of theatrical politics and economics that cost Whitbread his life and others their peace of mind hardly existed. His debut role as Shylock was speedily followed by another Shakespearean villain, King Richard the Third, on 12 February, a performance so strikingly full of genius and originality (notwithstanding Kean's debt to an earlier contemporary actor, George Frederick Cooke) that success, on his own importunate terms, was assured. Three more Shakespearean roles quickly appeared: Hamlet in mid-March and in May Othello and Iago on successive nights. For his benefit at the end of the month Kean displayed his first non-Shakespearean character to Drury Lane audiences, Luke in *Riches* (J. B. Burges' adaptation of Massinger's *The City Madam*). By traditional standards a dismal financial failure, Kean's benefit was in context a victory. Most benefits this season were disastrous for performers who, according to long-prevailing custom, were required to pay the 'charges', or operating costs of the theatre, before pocketing a shilling. In 1814 these charges amounted to £160,[4] and their ruinous effect on performers is clear in the nightly accounts. Well over a dozen actors and actresses posted deficiencies of as much as £120, while Kean, earning a net gain of £99, was outdistanced only by the peerless singer and perennial favourite, John Braham. Figures of this sort throw troublesome shadows on a financial picture highlighted by Kean's astonishing money-making prowess in Shakespearean roles. By 7 March his Richard III could produce a house of £643, a record broken five days later by the first performance of his Hamlet, which took in a phenomenal £660.[5]

[3] *Survey of London*, pp. 20–23.
[4] St. Vincent Troubridge, *The Benefit System in the British Theatre* (1967), p. 48.
[5] Drury Lane nightly accounts, 1813–14 (Folger Shakespeare Library).

Yet there was really no secret in Kean's attractiveness. Those who described his power over audiences did so in remarkably consistent terms. What makes Kean nevertheless difficult to assess is the very inconsistency of his style and manner almost invariably pointed out in notices of his triumphs. As F. G. Tomlins briefly put it, Kean's genius 'flashed with almost superhuman power amidst a mass of mannerisms, and occasional tricks, that only made it the more miraculous and irresistible'.[6] Clearly, the last thing anyone could have said of Kean was that he gave a seamless performance of whatever character he interpreted. Abrupt transitions, unexpected pauses, lightning descents from the grand to the col-loquial—these were the marks of his style, regardless of what he was playing. 'To see him act,' Coleridge observed in a now famous phrase, 'is like reading Shakspeare by flashes of lightning.'[7] The spasmodic nature of Kean's gesture and utterance would always draw attention, especially because, to many commentators, it called into question the whole relationship between artistic convention and life. One of Kean's greatest faults, according to one writer, was that 'he introduces much more "matter of fact"—or, as the people say, "Nature", than is compatible with scenic representation—He is like a poet who disdains metaphor'. . . .[8] Viewers seized on such qualities as extraordinary innovations or, alternatively, as intolerable subversions of tradition. 'He would reduce the character and language of the drama,' an observer noted, 'to what he calls the *level of real life*.'[9] In this forced conjunction of two realms, life and the stage, previously thought mutually exclusive, lay much of Kean's ability to surprise and fascinate audiences. His was a new emphasis whose time had apparently come.

Yet what held those audiences in conviction of his real genius

---

[6] *A Brief View of the English Drama* (1840), p. 75.

[7] *Specimens of the Table Talk of the Late Samuel Taylor Coleridge* (1835), I, 24.

[8] Unidentified clipping in Hawkins, I, f. 334.

[9] John Finlay, *Miscellanies* (Dublin, 1835), p. 210, quoted in Arthur Colby Sprague, *Shakespearian Players and Performances* (Cambridge, Mass., 1953), p. 74.

was another, more profound quality. Leigh Hunt, who denied that Kean possessed it, described the quality best, as 'something genuine and unconscious, something that moved, looked, and spoke solely under the impulse of the immediate idea'. . . .[10] 'His great merit,' a reviewer for *The Scotsman* found in 1817, 'consists in his having a soul which can not only be touched, but fired with passion, and a countenance which can indicate the most rapid changes of that soul.'[11] At a later date the actor George Vandenhoff explained the relationship of 'soul' and countenance that made Kean a true original. 'His style was impulsive,' Vandenhoff said, 'fitful, flashing, abounding in quick transitions; scarcely giving you time to think, but ravishing your wonder, and carrying you along with its impetuous rush and change of expression.' The delivery of Othelio's farewell 'ran on the same tones and semi-tones, had the same rests and breaks, the same *forte* and *piano*, the same *crescendo* and *diminuendo*, night after night, as if he spoke it from a musical score'. And, Vandenhoff went on, 'what beautiful, what thrilling music it was! the music of a broken heart—the cry of a despairing soul'.[12]

Kean's 'secret', if he had one, was the same as Garrick's and Kemble's and Siddons's: minute, tireless preparation of the role. The result exhibited on the stage, however, was inevitably different in the case of an actor temperamentally incapable of carrying on the 'grand tradition', particularly if it held the precedent for inveterate grace, neoclassic restraint, and only occasional bursts of ferocity set up by John Philip Kemble. Kean simply could not emulate stature of that sort. His appeal, and genius, lay elsewhere, as George Henry Lewes, that most perspicacious of playgoers, explained:

There was much in his performance of Othello which was spasmodic, slovenly, false. The address to the Senate was very bad. He had little

[10] *Leigh Hunt's Dramatic Criticism 1808–1831*, ed. L. H. and C. W. Houtchens (New York, 1949), p. 113.

[11] Clipping identified as 'Times, 1817' in Hawkins, II, f. 297.

[12] *Leaves from an Actor's Note Book* (New York, 1860), pp. 22–23, in Brander Matthews and Laurence Hutton, eds., *Actors and Actresses of Great Britain and the United States* (New York, 1886), II, 25.

power of elocution unless when sustained by a strong emotion; and this long simple narrative was the kind of speech he could not manage at all. He gabbled over it, impatient to arrive at the phrase 'And this is all the witchcraft I have used. Here comes the lady, let her witness it.' His delivery of this 'point' always startled the audience into applause by its incisive tone and its abrupt transition; yet nothing could be more out of keeping with the Shakspearian character. [In the first and second acts] Kean's Othello was rather irritating and disappointing—arresting the mind but not satisfying it. From the third act onwards all was wrought out with a mastery over the resources of expression such as has been seldom approached. In the successive unfolding of these great scenes he represented with incomparable effect the lion-like fury, the deep and haggard pathos, the forlorn sense of desolation, alternating with gusts of stormy cries for vengeance, the misgivings and sudden reassurances, the calm and deadly resolution of one not easily moved, but who, being moved, was stirred to the very depths.[13] (Plate 6)

The pattern, described by Lewes, of increasing audience rapport in Kean's Othello was repeated in his other roles. Tricky and flashy as he was, ready to leap at the opportunity for an ingenious new reading or an unorthodox gesture, no audience could long remain unmoved. It was impossible, as Lewes acknowledged, to observe him 'without being strangely shaken by the terror, and the pathos, and the passion of a stormy spirit uttering itself in tones of irresistible power'.[14]

Kean was, then, an obvious and extravagant innovator. Still, to speak of innovation, as so many of his contemporaries did, is to view the present as the latest point of continuity with the past. For all his unorthodoxy, his flagrant violation of theatrical propriety, Kean's appearance made solid contact with an acting tradition very much alive. The art of Kemble was still vigorous and in regular evidence at the rival theatre, from which that actor would not retire until 1817. His sister Mrs. Siddons had bade her farewells in 1812, only two years before Kean's Drury Lane debut. And to look back to their own debuts is to survey in the process most of the last quarter of the eighteenth century. Not long before that came the retirement

---

[13] *On Actors and the Art of Acting* (1875), pp. 5–6.   [14] *On Actors*, p. 3.   61

of Garrick after his own quarter-century and more of dominating London audiences, and before him—to name only some of the most prominent—were Quin and Booth, Bracegirdle and Betterton.

From the time of the Restoration, in fact, an unbroken tradition of acting, true child of a vital repertory theatre, had graced the English stage. When Kean's latter-day star shone in the ascendant, an entire, homogeneous set of methods and assumptions was once again illuminated. Notwithstanding his posture as a maverick, defying conventional readings of major roles and hurling implied insult at styles once serviceable but apparently out of date, Kean had as much in common with his predecessors as any debutant in the history of the art.

Aside from the audiences themselves, the two great constants in the English theatre of Kean's age were the plays that appeared year in, year out and the actors who performed them. Consequently a certain number of classic roles were played again and again, and every aspiring actor or actress cut his or her teeth on them and carried a working knowledge of them to the end of a long (or short) career. The orientation of the theatrical event towards the actor in character is unmistakable in all the evidence of theatrical life that survives from the period, most notably in the playbills. Virtually never is the dramatist's name mentioned. If the play is an established repertory piece, everyone knows who he is; if a new play, no one seems to care, although theatrical gossip in newspapers and elsewhere may spread some word. The bill will simply state: *The Tragedy of King Lear*, King Lear: Mr. Garrick; or *Venice Preserv'd*, Jaffier: Mr. Barry, Belvidera: Mrs. Barry; or *The Tragedy of Coriolanus*, Coriolanus: Mr. Kemble, Volumnia: Mrs. Siddons, and so on with the rest of the cast. Audiences by and large did not go to the theatre to see Shakespeare or Congreve, Jonson or Sheridan as such; the notion is far too abstract. Rather, they went to see Betterton as Hamlet, Mrs. Siddons as Zara in Congreve's *The Mourning Bride*, Garrick as Abel Drugger in his adaptation of *The Alchemist*, or Mrs. Jordan as Miss Hoyden in Sheridan's *A Trip to Scarborough*. Massinger was of no particular interest in himself, but London audiences flocked to see Kean's Sir Giles Overreach all the same (Plate 7). It was expected, of course, that the entire play would be well cast and that a good deal of ensemble playing would happily coexist with a somewhat greater emphasis on leading roles.

These factors together created the strong tradition of individual interpretation that is the hallmark of English acting. The vitality of that tradition may be judged even by theatregoers of our own day, as in the case of Laurence Olivier's Othello (National Theatre, 1964). The apparent deracination of Olivier's character from conventional theatrical identity to a controversially topical and very dark-skinned West Indian really does not obscure its precedent in the romantically flamboyant character played by Edmund Kean.[15] At the same time, of course, one understands that the repertory theatre as it existed in Kean's day has left only a thin shadow of itself in a few modern companies. In that earlier time there were essentially only two theatres in London except for a summer house, the little Haymarket, and theatrical life was both highly circumscribed and tightly regulated. In effect, one acted at Drury Lane or Covent Garden or nowhere, except out of season or out of London. There were consequently two places where Shakespeare and the other classics of the English stage could be seen to best advantage, and these two houses were open rivals, occasionally performing the same play on the same night. No wonder, then, that audiences grew intimately familiar with a relatively small number of roles. No wonder also that many playgoers came to the theatre with eyes incisively critical, ready to compare the present actor or actress with his or her rival at the other theatre or even in the same company, and also against predecessors still held in living memory.

The result, in the performer's approach to the role, was an extensive search for originality of detail to highlight and perhaps modify the familiar outline of the character. Where the same words in the same order formed the basic continuity,

[15] It is noteworthy that the programme for the Olivier Othello at the Old Vic, containing a section on previous interpretations of the role, features Kean prominently.

it was left to the performer to introduce new shades of meaning or even an entirely new concept of the role by means of changes of vocal inflection, pauses, gesture, movement—'business' in general. In short, it was expected that the performer would exert his or her own special claim to the audience's attention. The force of a unique personality, exhibited within the reassuringly familiar confines of the art, was what audiences paid their money to see.

Hardly a better means could have been contrived for preserving the competent player while yet giving scope to genius. Although no formal links existed between the London theatres and those of the provinces, a system of interchangeable elements had grown up which insured the survival of dramatic tradition. When Kean came to Drury Lane from the Theatre Royal at Exeter he brought with him a player's practical knowledge, not only of a series of roles, Shakespearean and otherwise, that he was prepared to act instantly or on short notice, but a certain *savoir faire* that made it easy for him or anyone else trained in the 'school' of the provincial theatre to step in and give a smooth, professional performance with a minimum of rehearsal (often simply a brief run-through to set cues; the actor's part was his own concern). He knew, for example—no one knew better—how to 'take the stage', as the great Joseph Jefferson later described that particular clap-trap: the actor 'would take the stage with tremendous strides from the center to the extreme right or left after making a point, thereby signifying to the audience that if they desired to applaud *that* was their time'.[16] He knew how to use the stage wings to make an effective entrance or exit, how to pace a speech or frame a quick retort for maximum audience response. His talent was wonderful for making his auditors think that what he did came on the spur of the inspired moment. As Lewes explained, however, nothing in his role was left to chance, for 'Kean vigilantly and patiently rehearsed every detail, trying the tones until his ear was satisfied, practicing looks and gestures until his artistic sense was

[16] *The Autobiography of Joseph Jefferson*, ed. Alan S. Downer (Cambridge, Mass., 1964), p. 53.

satisfied; and having once regulated these he never changed them'. In fact, 'when Kean was rehearsing on a new stage he accurately counted the number of steps he had to take before reaching a certain spot, or before uttering a certain word; these steps were justly regarded by him as part of the mechanism which could no more be neglected than the accompaniment to an air could be neglected by a singer'.[17]

Although Kean was undoubtedly more thorough than the average repertory actor, these were the commonplace efforts made by performers in the exercise of their craft. What separated the actor of genius from his workaday contemporary was not only a less finite capacity for taking such pains but a sense of the human implications of the new business that were the stock in trade of everyone who pretended to competence.

The role of Richard the Third—in the standard playing text, Colley Cibber's ruthless redaction of Shakespeare's panoramic history play—offers a lucid example. Garrick's triumph in the character in his debut of 1741 established his own superiority and virtuosity of style as an actor; at the time, he made the role of Richard an unavoidable test for subsequent actors. Moreover, Garrick's fresh interpretation of the character set a standard for humane understanding of a supposedly detestable villain that remained long after Garrick's retirement from the stage. As Garrick's biographer Percy Fitzgerald later remarked, audiences were struck by the actor's total departure from the previous 'broad conventional delineation of "the wicked tyrant", who was savage and furious, nothing more, merely raging like a maniac'. Consequently Garrick's behaviour in the battle scenes, where he was 'as loud, fierce, and furious as could be desired',[18] was coloured by the new understanding of the man himself that informed the entire presentation.

The interpretations of Richard presented by later actors depended squarely on Garrick's precedent, whether they followed it strictly or not. Kemble, who could not really look

[17] *On Actors*, pp. 7–8.
[18] Percy Fitzgerald, *The Life of David Garrick*, rev. edn. (1889), pp. 250–251. See also George Winchester Stone, Jr., 'Bloody, Cold, and Complex Richard: David Garrick's Interpretation', in *On Stage and Off*, ed. John W. Ehrstine *et al.* (Pullman, Wash., 1968), pp. 14–25.

the part of a villain and so emphasized his own great strong point, a flawless nobility of voice and carriage, nevertheless followed Garrick's portrayal of ultimate heroism: 'When he felt his death-wound, he seemed rather to throw life away, than to wait till it was wrested from him', and 'he bounded ere he fell, as if to leap into eternity, and there seize the renown he had won in spite of fate or fortune'.[19] George Frederick Cooke brought almost completely opposite qualities to the role; his 'subtle, ludicrous, sarcastic turns' were constantly pointed out.[20] Yet Cooke evidently shared Kemble's notion that the villain's last moments proclaim the essence of the man. As one reviewer explained, 'The ineffectual struggle to catch, in his expiring moments, at his fallen sword, was well conceived, and in the true spirit of Richard, whom even his enemies affirmed to have been "a noble knight, who defended himself to the *last breath*, with eminent valour".'[21] Unlike Kean, Cooke tended to vary the details of his performance. Once in the dying scene, his Richard made an effort to rise but, failing, thrust his sword despairingly away. Another time he dropped the sword and, attempting to recover it, fell again. These moments, his critic thought, were nevertheless 'equally characteristic of the intrepid furious Richard' who, at the very end, rising on an elbow, turns on his adversary Richmond a countenance that 'was terrible, it had soul in it; it looked a testamentary curse'. . . .

By implication—verified by still other reviews—Cooke had departed to a degree from the overtly sympathetic rendering of the character by Garrick and Kemble. The concluding business with the sword, however, remained indicative of the fierce intrepidity common to Garrick's, Kemble's and then Cooke's presentations, while at the same time Cooke had infused into it a new sense of an inveterate, half-sublime yet deeply malignant spirit, a quality reflecting the more complex notions of heroic villains emerging at the time in contemporary Gothic drama.

[19] [H. Martin], *Remarks on Mr. John Kemble's Performance of Hamlet and Richard the Third* (1802), p. 38.

[20] *Monthly Mirror*, 10 (1800), p. 319.

[21] *Monthly Mirror*, 10 (1800), p. 321.

Consequently, in the tradition which began with Garrick, much of Cooke's Richard is recapitulated in Kean's portrayal. Like Cooke, Kean was utterly unfit to play the sort of hauteur and, some thought, frigid stoicism that Kemble brought to such roles as Cato and Coriolanus and introduced (perhaps inappropriately) into Richard when he performed the role tradition had made compulsory. Yet Kean could summon up his own brand of unyielding superiority, especially to those unfortunate circumstances of life that, in the Romantic theatre, invariably make for tragedy. In Kean's death as Richard, said the journalist Thomas Barnes,

he fights desperately: he is disarmed, and exhausted of all bodily strength: he disdains to fall, and his strong volition keeps him standing: he fixes that head, full of intellectual and heroic power, directly on his enemy: he bears up his chest with an expansion, which seems swelling with more than human spirit: he holds his uplifted arm in calm but dreadful defiance of his conqueror. But he is but man, and he falls after this sublime effort senseless to the ground.[22]

The description is extravagant but not untypical of even the best theatre critic of the age, Hazlitt, who said that Kean's death scene as Richard 'had a preternatural and terrific grandeur, as if his will could not be disarmed, and the very phantoms of his despair had a withering power'.[23]

There is no doubt, then, of Kean's reliance on a living tradition virtually as old as the professional theatre in England, just as no doubt exists of his own virtuosity in moulding it to his own capabilities. The vitality of this tradition is evident in the relatively slow but steady accumulation of 'business' passed on from one actor or actress to another. It is clear also in an even more basic phenomenon, an assumption about the very nature of acting, that had existed at least from the time of Betterton. The preoccupation by actor and critic alike with the details of a performance could not have continued, decade after decade, if players and audiences were not agreed upon the relationship between general human nature, considered in the abstract, and its formal embodiment on a stage.

[22] Thomas Barnes, review in the *Examiner*, 27 February 1814, p. 139.
[23] Hazlitt, V, 182.

The legacy inherited by early nineteenth-century actors, and audiences, from the previous age was, simply stated, that every human emotion has its commonly recognized manifestation in outward behaviour. Despite the chaotic variety of commentary on the art of acting published in England since the days of Queen Anne, there was widespread agreement that the 'language' of an actor's performance—movement, gesture, intonation, and so on—imitated a universal language of the passions. Admittedly, a century-long argument had taken place over whether the aspirant begins by learning the conventions of the stage player or by confronting the reality of his own emotions, a debate brilliantly examined by Diderot in his *Paradoxe sur le Comédien*.[24] Significant as such controversy was, it cannot obscure the fundamental tendency of all acting, up through the age of Kean, towards consistent objectification. That is to say, it was believed that human emotions, whatever their source, could be formally presented on the stage in the full range and intensity found in human nature itself. Moreover, a process of simplification clearly discriminated the outward signs of these emotions from one another, making them instantly recognizable from all points in the auditorium.

For example, according to commonplace tragic convention, an expression of defiance began at the boots, travelled upwards to the top of the head, then down again to its origin.[25] Similarly, according to an early nineteenth-century handbook of acting, the action of dismissing someone with approval is done with 'the right hand open, gently waved toward the person'; if the dismissal is done with displeasure, 'the hand is hastily thrown out toward the person dismissed, the back part towards him, the countenance at the same time turned away from him'.[26] The purpose of such gestures is not subtlety, of

[24] See Joseph W. Donohue, Jr., *Dramatic Character in the English Romantic Age* (Princeton, 1970), pp. 216–223, and the scholarship cited there and on pp. 359–363.

[25] Charles Dickens, *Nicholas Nickleby*, Chap. 29.

[26] *The Theatrical Speaker; or an Elucidation of the Whole Science of Acting*, 2nd edn. (1807), p. 19, quoted in Conrad Joy Bishop, 'Melodramatic Acting: Concept and Technique in the Performance of Early Nineteenth Century English Melodrama', Diss. Stanford, 1967, p. 70.

course, but clarity. And yet a system of apparently rigid conventions of this sort is susceptible to a great range of emotion and even a profundity of expression, especially when familiar, straightforward gesture or attitude was enhanced by specific business. In Edward Moore's tragedy *The Gamester* (1753), the despair of the hero Beverley is described in this way: 'When all was lost, he fixt his Eyes upon the Ground, and stood some Time, with folded Arms, stupid and motionless. Then snatching his Sword, that hung against the Wainscot, he sat him down; and with a Look of fixt Attention, drew Figures on the Floor.'[27] In context, Beverley's idle sketching on the floor with the point of his sword becomes an expression of purposelessness. Kean's adoption of this 'business' in another situation, however, might well have been genuinely illuminating. Kean's Richard the Third, just before the tent scene and its presentation of the terrors of conscience, stands in a kind of reverie, 'drawing lines upon the ground with the point of his sword'....[28] It seems likely that Kean's innovation was meant to convey an almost unconscious revelation by the character that no hope, either of victory or survival, remained.[29]

Although a later writer could complain that the 'points' made by actors through the invention of stage business substituted the playing of tricks for the playing of characters,[30] show and substance could be closely allied. A more telling objection was often aimed at the exaggeration of voice and manner that, by the time of Kean's advent, did consistent duty as conventionalized reality. Two comments on the acting style of Henry Johnstone set the issue in perspective and at the same time illustrate the relatively extreme nature of the melodramatic acting evident on early nineteenth-century stages. Leigh Hunt, writing in 1807, decided that Johnstone's acting was inappropriately exaggerated, always having an

[27] Moore, *The Gamester. A Tragedy* (1753), Act IV, p. 53.
[28] *Hunt's Dramatic Criticism*, p. 114.
[29] See the discussion of this point in Donohue, *Dramatic Character*, pp. 347–348.
[30] Leman Thomas Rede, *The Road to the Stage* (1827), p. 94.

important air no matter what the character. 'He indulges himself in all the mute cant of the stage,' Hunt charged; 'he rolls his eyes, frowns most terrifically, looks downwards on one side with a swelling front and in an attitude of still contempt, prepares us for every trifling speech with cold pauses of intended meaning.'[31] Such behaviour was praised, however, by an earlier critic who found the style exactly suitable for melodrama. As the villain Romaldi in Holcroft's *A Tale of Mystery*, Johnstone's bearing and gestures were 'admirably varied to the transitions of the scene, and the boldness and rapidity of his attitudes and actions evinced a perfect knowledge of this difficult branch of the art'.[32]

Undoubtedly, most acting of this sort could, from a modern perspective, be called melodramatic. It is a style that appears consistent with the kind of vividly overstated manner alleged to be common at certain minor theatres: 'If a character asked for a piece of bread and cheese he would raise and lower his eyebrows three times, pause between each word, which was dragged up from the very pit of his stomach, and intoned as tragically as though he had requested a cup of poison.'[33] Certainly, melodramatic acting was characterized by vocal exaggeration and by 'quick and stirring actions' growing out of an expertise in pantomime.[34] But it should be understood that the words *natural* and *unnatural*, ubiquitous in the critical praise and blame of the age, were not used to distinguish melodramatic acting from some other, supposedly less extreme, style. They were used simply to indicate approval or disapproval. What remains clear about the nature of acting in

---

[31] *Critical Essays on the Performers of the London Theatres* (1807), p. 39, quoted by Gloria Estelle Mandeville, 'A Century of Melodrama on the London Stage, 1790–1890', Diss. Columbia, 1954, p. 92.

[32] *The Times*, 15 November 1802, quoted in Mandeville, 'A Century of Melodrama', p. 92.

[33] Baker, p. 317.

[34] See *The Amateur, or Guide to the Stage* (Philadelphia & New York, n.d.), p. 51, quoted in Bishop, 'Melodramatic Acting', p. 136, and the praise of Charles Farley, director of pantomimes for Covent Garden, for his mute action as Francisco in *A Tale of Mystery*, in the *Morning Post*, 15 November 1802, quoted in Mandeville, 'A Century of Melodrama', p. 93.

Kean's day is that the development of melodramatic acting which took place at this time was an extension in degree, not a change in kind.

Granted, the degree could be quite extreme. Charles Durang describes a 'mad melodramatic hero' of the period as 'bellowing in spasmodic declamation, roaring like the bull of Bashan, developing passion in distortions of face and body . . . ranting out the words as if to drown the sounds of the orchestra'.[35] And yet, early and late, actors in traditional tragedy employed a certain distortion of 'natural' speech for reasons of special emphasis. As early as 1800, for example, a reviewer of the Othello of Pope, playing opposite Cooke's Iago, points out that this actor 'almost ludicrously ends every break of the voice to the tune of "*a* down *a*"; I will *a*—revenge *a*, &c. and invariably uses *ye* and *you* with the broad Dutch pronunciation "*yaw*—"'. Similarly, Charles Kean's debut performance as Norval in *Douglas* was criticized for the actor's 'drawling pronunciation': 'Tremble he pronounces *terremble*, increase *inker-rease*, and many other words in the same barbarous manner.'[36] Such exaggeration became one of the common features of melodramatic acting. Whether found at the Surrey or Drury Lane, however, deliberate vocal distortion had its legitimate uses. John Palmer, for example, in Charles Lamb's perceptive description, could switch instantly from one voice to another 'more decisively histrionic', a voice designed to mark things out 'in a sort of italics' and so enhance the audience's comic enjoyment of superiority over the rest of the characters.[37]

Much of our knowledge of acting in this period comes from such detailed commentary, focusing consistently on the chief roles of the play. In a contemporary observer's view, an audience found it hard to believe in the illusion of the scene 'unless our imagination is a good deal assisted by the principal

[35] 'The Philadelphia Stage; from 1749 to 1821', Philadelphia *Sunday Dispatch* (1854–56), Chaps. 58 and 64 (n.p.), quoted in Bishop, 'Melodramatic Acting', p. 77.
[36] Unidentified clipping in Hawkins, III, f. 242.
[37] 'On Some of the Old Actors', in Lamb, II, 140.

person of the drama',[38] and the marked propensity of criticism is to concentrate exclusively on the star performer. And yet, to view Kean in relation to his theatrical surroundings is to place him, not on an empty stage, but on one peopled by a company of actors and actresses who share the same sources of strong precedent and opportunity for change. Kean succeeded as a 'star', and in fact was instrumental in advancing the 'star system' and its emphasis on a single actor and its consequent and unfortunate depreciation of ensemble acting. Even so, Kean could not have achieved what he did without depending extensively on the resources of the traditional acting company.

The basic idea of this company, later called the 'stock company', was of a permanent, self-sufficient group of players ready and able to act an old play or a new one. The composition of the company, basically unchanged from the time of the Restoration or even before to the disappearance of stock companies in the late nineteenth century, depended on the existence of acting specialities, called 'lines of business', which identified both the relationship of the characters in the play and the correlative usefulness of the members of the company. The specialities articulated by the scheme included, in roughly descending order, a *leading man* for principal roles in tragedy and melodrama; a *juvenile* who also typically served as a *light comedian*, playing fine gentlemen and lovers; a *heavy*—perhaps more than one—for the villains and middle-aged men; an *old man*, again possibly more than one; an *eccentric comedian*, later referred to as a *character actor*; the *low comedian*, who portrayed the Tony Lumpkins and other broadly rendered characters; several *walking gentlemen*—the Benvolios and Balthasars of the play; and one or more *utility men*, whose usefulness lay precisely in their lack of specialization and who consequently could fill almost any miscellaneous role not covered by their colleagues. The female lines of business, although not so numerous, were of the same complementary nature. There was a *leading lady*; a *second lady*, *juvenile lead* or, as the term is still used today, an *ingénue*; an *old woman*; possibly a *female heavy* in addition; the pert, perhaps hoydenish actress

[38] Unidentified clipping dated [December 1817] in Hawkins, II, f. 282.

who played chambermaids and other such roles, known today as the *soubrette*; a *walking lady*; possibly a *character actress*; and, of course, a female *utility*. In addition, depending on the needs of the particular play, supernumeraries, or 'supers', would be hired (or simply persuaded) to walk on, spear or handkerchief in hand, to swell a progress or enhance an atmosphere. By definition they were not part of the regular company. As the nineteenth century progressed, these lines of business became more and more rigid and specialized, but the basic concept remained unchanged.[39]

Matching the typical members of the repertory company against the *dramatis personae* of *Hamlet* indicates at once how serviceable the arrangement was. Alongside the tragedian playing Hamlet there would range the heavy as King Claudius, the old man as Polonius, a walking gentleman as Horatio, the juvenile as Laertes, and several more walking gentlemen for Rosencrantz and Guildenstern, while the eccentric comedian would play Osric, the low comedian the first gravedigger, and the utility man the second, with other walking gentlemen or utilities as officers, soldiers, and players. A second old man would do well as the Player King and could easily double as the Ghost, while Fortinbras, usually no problem at all because he was regularly cut out of the play (as were Voltemand and Cornelius), could theoretically be taken up by a walking gentleman or perhaps a second juvenile who had fallen on hard times. As for the female members of the company, although their range would not be fully drawn on in a Shakespearean tragedy, the leading lady would doubtless play Gertrude, while the female juvenile would perform Ophelia and certain walking gentlewomen would as a matter of course appear in selected scenes.

For some of these actors and actresses, such small, relatively unnoticed roles were stepping-stones to higher things. For others, like the utility man in the Dickensian acting troupe managed by Vincent Crummles, they were a way of life. Miss

[39] See Edward William Mammen, *The Old Stock Company School of Acting* (Boston, 1945), p. 20, and Sybil Rosenfeld's article 'Stock Company', *Oxford Companion to the Theatre*, 3rd edn. (1967).

73

Snevellicci's papa, who 'had been in the profession ever since he had first played the ten-year-old imps in the Christmas pantomimes', was a man 'who could sing a little, dance a little, fence a little, act a little, and do everything a little, but not much; who had been sometimes in the ballet, and sometimes in the chorus, at every theatre in London; who was always selected in virtue of his figure to play the military visitors and the speechless noblemen; who always wore a smart dress, and came on arm-in-arm with a smart lady in short petticoats,—and always did it too with such an air that people in the pit had been several times known to cry out "Bravo!" under the impression that he was somebody.'[40] It was well to be content with such parts, for as a contemporary observer pointed out, 'once establish a name for utility, and you throw down all hopes of eminence in the profession'.[41]

Movement up through the ranks was still very much a normal thing, as the career of John Fawcett illustrates. Fawcett began his London career with a debut at Covent Garden in 1791 as Caleb in Pilon's comedy *He Would be a Soldier*, initiating a modest reputation for eccentric comedy. Then in 1798 he replaced John Bannister as comic hero at the Haymarket and so assumed a larger range of parts than those available at Covent Garden. He prospered and, in 1800, became acting manager, his reputation secure enough that, by 1807, Leigh Hunt could observe that if dramatic authors wish to portray 'a gabbling humourist' they necessarily copy Fawcett's manner.[42] By 1825, however, Fawcett had abandoned the country fellows and eccentric light comedy parts of his earlier days, despite their popularity, and was concentrating on old men. A contemporary appraiser thought him second in this only to the renowned Dowton, despite Fawcett's lack of 'oily humour' and 'warmth of colouring', since his humorousness was exclusively his own; he never stooped to grimace or ribaldry. This critic goes on to discriminate between two sub-specialities of Fawcett's old men, his 'singing

[40] *Nicholas Nickleby*, Chap. 30.
[41] *Oxberry's Dramatic Biography* (1825), II, 95.
[42] *Critical Essays*, p. vii.

old men'—perhaps the best on the stage for 'pedantic assumption, stiffness of manner, and loquacity'—and his 'feeling old men'. In the latter roles, such as Job Thornberry in the younger Colman's *John Bull*, he 'goes to the heart without effort', never degenerating into pompous tragedy, always felicitously intermingling comic touches.[43]

As played by Fawcett and others, the role of the countryman is one of the best examples from the contemporary stage of the happy wedding of comic acting talent and vigorous, familiar characterization. In addition to Fawcett, at least three other early nineteenth-century actors made partial or entire careers for themselves in such roles as Goldsmith's Tony Lumpkin, Frank Oatland in Thomas Morton's *A Cure for the Heart-Ache*, Jacob Gawkey in Sophia Lee's *Chapter of Accidents*, and Andrew in James Kenney's *Love, Law, and Physic*. John Emery, who first delighted London audiences at Covent Garden in 1798, had, it was said, no competitor in playing rustics. 'What expression lived in his light blue eye!' exclaimed the writer of a retrospective account in 1825, 'what meaning in his vacant countenance!'[44] John Liston, after making himself a favourite in some of the country boys at Newcastle-upon-Tyne, first appeared in London at the Haymarket in 1805 as Sheepface in William Macready's *The Village Lawyer*, after which he swiftly moved on to Covent Garden, taking with him a wonderful 'happy negativeness' of face, a true picture of 'obtuse intellect'.[45] A new, ostensibly more sophisticated treatment of these roles appeared subsequently in the acting of Edward Knight, whose debut took place with the Drury Lane company performing in temporary quarters at the Lyceum in 1809. 'His country boys,' observed a contemporary biographer, 'are never unsophisticated, artless clowns; they are shrewd, designing, knowing lads; instead of rustic simplicity, we have metropolitan shrugs and winks; in the place of a lax gait and dangling arms, round shoulders, &c., he has as precise a walk, and as prim a figure, as a pedagogue might require; add to

[43] *Oxberry's Dramatic Biography*, II, 40–46.
[44] *Oxberry's Dramatic Biography*, II, 220.
[45] *Oxberry's Dramatic Biography*, I, 18–19.

this, his vicious habit of perpetual laughter' . . .[46] (Plate 10).

In the context of the stock company system, the success of an actor or actress inevitably meant the virtual ownership of many if not all of the roles encompassed by his or her line of business. The stability of the arrangement could prove a disadvantage to the newcomer, as Ralph Sherwin discovered, to his great disappointment, in 1823. After a long apprenticeship in provincial theatres, Sherwin was engaged to play country men at Drury Lane. His debut role was, appropriately, Dandie Dinmont in *Guy Mannering*, but in the next two years he was able to secure only this part and two others, since Knight 'was in possession' of almost every role Sherwin wanted to play.[47]

It was consequently necessary for the management to keep extensive records of their players' dramatic property. Such a record, reflecting the distribution of roles at Drury Lane in the years after Kean's appearance there, survives in a large bound volume now in the Folger Shakespeare Library. The smallest number of parts, eighteen, belongs to Kean himself, a fact indicative of his exclusive position as first tragedian (although some few of the roles are in comedies) and also of his notoriously narrow range. Elliston, to take another example, could play such Kean roles as Hamlet, Othello, and Octavian in the younger Colman's *The Mountaineers* while on other nights impersonating the great range of comic heroes from Benedick in *Much Ado About Nothing* and Archer in *The Beaux' Stratagem* to Young Dornton in Morton's *The Road to Ruin* and Rover in O'Keeffe's *Wild Oats*, for a total of some forty-six characters. The interlocking nature of lines of business is clear once again in the roles of Alexander Rae, a young pretender to first tragic roles who could step in as Hamlet, Jaffier, Othello, Octavian and Romeo, who in addition knew and sometimes played other romantic heroes like Douglas, George Barnwell, Beverley in *The Gamester* and Prince Hal, but who also had an extensive repertoire of such second-line juveniles as Richmond in *Richard the Third*, Bassanio in *The Merchant of Venice*, Macduff in

[46] *Oxberry's Dramatic Biography*, II, 115.
[47] *Oxberry's Dramatic Biography*, I, 184.

Macbeth and Hastings in *Jane Shore*: some thirty-seven roles in all. Among less flexible specialities are the more than thirty old men, headed by Polonius, of Munden and the twenty-three stage Irishmen of Johnstone. And at the other end of the spectrum it is unsurprising but none the less impressive to see some eighty-two roles assigned to the utility man Chatterley, comprising a collection of generic characters whose occupations delineate the great range of common humanity represented on the contemporary stage: sailor, fiddler, smuggler, servant, gipsy, waiter, tapster, carrier, sentinel, post boy, bailiff, robber, porter, stockbroker, clown, watchman, officer, murderer, groom, peasant and 'Frenchman'. Among the female members of the company, demarcations are clearly drawn between the roles of the heroines played by Mrs. Bartley—the Isabellas, Juliets, Portias, Lady Randolphs, Euphrasias and Belvideras—and the old women enumerated in Mrs. Sparks's Mrs. Hardcastle, Mrs. Malaprop, Mistress Quickly, Juliet's nurse and their less immortal sisters.

In the context of the legitimate dramatic repertory, then, the stock company organization was the obviously efficient way to make available to nightly audiences the great variety of plays in the tradition, together with the new pieces not infrequently added. As the nineteenth century moved on, however, the arrangement became ever less satisfactory, so far as the great houses of Drury Lane and Covent Garden were concerned. Writing in 1840, by which time the tendency and its attendant difficulties had become quite clear, F. G. Tomlins outlined the ruinous cost of efforts to please the heterogeneous groups that only together could fill such large theatres. The very specialities that permit the performance of a large number of plays at short notice, he explained, also make it necessary to hire what are, in effect, three or even four companies of performers: one for comedy and tragedy, another for melodrama and pantomime, a large and very expensive opera company, and still another set of performers for spectacle and ballet.[48]

Surviving records bear out the justice of Tomlins' observation. For example, the company hired by Drury Lane

[48] Tomlins, *Brief View of the English Drama*, p. 109.

77

for 1812–13, the first season in the new theatre, numbered forty-two actors, twenty-five actresses, nine male 'Figure Dancers', nine female dancers, and a chorus of fifteen.[49] A similar listing for the same theatre for the 1827–28 season gives an almost identical number of forty-one actors and twenty-five actresses.[50]

The stability, not to say rigidity, of the repertory system is evident in these figures, but it is clear also that such a system worked, if at all, only on balance, over a full season of frequent changes in bill that engage in turn the talents of the entire company. The long-running success of some one piece, whether a tragedy, pantomime, opera, or ballet spectacle, created an anomalous situation in which a disproportionate number of performers, almost all of them hired by the season and paid by the week whether they appeared or not, sat idle. Meanwhile the minor theatres, with their smaller companies and developing house specialities, could be run more economically and efficiently even aside from the lower salaries that prevailed there. At the Adelphi, the playwright Douglas Jerrold pointed out in 1832, one could see the whole company in a single night's entertainment, while at Drury Lane or Covent Garden not even one-third would be in evidence. 'They split upon that very rock,' Jerrold said.[51]

To many minds, including that of Bulwer, chairman of the 1832 parliamentary committee inquiring into the causes of the decline of the drama, the cause of these ills and others as well was the system of theatrical monopoly itself. In replying to Bulwer's question whether the monopoly was oppressive to the actor, J. P. Collier gave the concrete example of the winter theatre manager who says to his performers, 'I will not engage you next season if you act at any minor theatre.' These performers had no recourse, since they preferred engagements at winter theatres even under such tyrannous disadvantage.[52]

The implication was that a *laissez-faire* policy would allow

[49] List of Drury Lane company, 1812–13 (Folger Shakespeare Library).
[50] Unidentified clipping dated [23 September 1827] in Hawkins, III, f. 238.
[51] *Report*, Qq. 1903–9.
[52] *Report*, Q. 402.

both great and good actors to find their own level, with a resultant benefit to all—not only to minor metropolitan theatres, in fact, but to the theatres of the provinces. According to George Bartley, stage manager at Covent Garden, the melodrama that flourished at London's minor theatres was causing the disappearance of the provincial theatre as a school for actors. A case in point is the Bath theatre, Bartley explained. When Elliston acted there, prior to his appearance in London, it would have suited the manager's purpose to let him play Othello or Benedick three or four times in a season, but since the provincial theatres had begun performing the 'time-serving, popular dramas' of the minor houses, such opportunities were gone. At Bath and elsewhere 'they only play novelties'.[53] On the other hand, some thought that the minor theatres had supplanted the country playhouses as a school for actors and that the consequent deterioration of acting, and of the acting profession, was traceable to the legal restrictions still in force at these houses.

The profession of actor, F. G. Tomlins concluded, was the worst an intellectual man could at that time select. 'Its requisites are more various, its difficulties greater, its remuneration (except to an exorbitantly paid few) worse, and more uncertain, and its duties more harassing, than those of any other,' he said, while in addition it suffers from a certain religious prejudice. The intellectual actor must, at his manager's will, associate 'with horses and wild beasts', and the custom of actors' benefits forces him to partake in losses but never allows a share in gains. In recent times, Tomlins went on, the disproportionate value placed on the leading performer entails the sacrifice of subordinate roles to enhance his own. Moreover, such plays, as performed in the cavernous reaches of the patent houses, unhappily seduce the performer into 'rant and exaggeration'. What it all came down to, Tomlins implied, was the loss of a balanced, ensemble mode of playing, 'the combination of an intelligent set of actors, who can relish and express the merits of the author'.[54]

[53] *Report*, Qq. 3259–60.
[54] *Brief View of the English Drama*, pp. 113–117.

No doubt, the growing tendency of audiences was to seek pleasure in the player more than the play. Charles Lamb recalled 'how we *once* used to read a Play Bill—not, as now peradventure, singling out a favourite performer, and casting a negligent eye over the rest; but spelling out every name, down to the very mutes and servants of the scene'. . . .[55] The result was the paradox that third-rate or fourth-rate characters were often indifferently played—'bad and careless acting of the *subs* mars the whole business', said one reviewer of the Covent Garden company[56]—but that the age was nevertheless one of great actors. The Covent Garden company of 1808 was the best ever assembled, according to a later proprietor, John Forbes, who named such illustrious members as Kemble, his younger brother Charles, Cooke, Lewis, Incledon, Munden, Fawcett, Young, Emery, Liston, Mrs. Siddons and others.[57] Still, only a few members of that stellar company were likely to be on stage at a given time, or even on a given night. Moreover, their roles and perquisites, purchased at such large human cost and against great odds, were jealously guarded.

A letter of 1822 from Kean to Elliston, then manager of Drury Lane, captures the essence of the situation. Elliston's treasurer had written to inform Kean that Charles Mayne Young, a rising tragedian, had been hired by Drury Lane for thirty nights and that consequently Kean was wanted to act opposite him. With typical panache and arrogance Kean sent a hot retort to Elliston:

Now this I call exceeding imprudent, & I hope without your authority.—the Throne is mine. I will maintain it—even at the expence of expatriation—go where I will I shall always bear it with me—& even if I sail to another quarter of the globe, no man in this profession can rob me of the character of the first English Actor. When I come to London Elliston I open in Richard the 3^d my second character *Othello*!! Hamlet—Lear—& so go through my general cast, if Mr Young is ambitious to act with me—he must commence with

[55] 'On some of the Old Actors', in Lamb, II, 132.
[56] Unidentified clipping dated [January 1830] in Hawkins, III, f. 320.
[57] *Report*, Q. 1920.

Iago.—& when the whole of *my* characters is exhausted we may then turn our thoughts—to Cymbeline, & Venice Preserved—at the same time I do not wish to influence your Dramatic Politicks, if you think M[r] Young will answer your purpose better than me

Verbum sat—
Vale.[58]

By his own metaphor a monarch, Kean was by common consent a 'star' as well. In more recent usage the term refers to any theatrical luminary, but in the early nineteenth century it had the more specialized meaning of an actor or actress hired by a theatre on the short term as a special attraction. Initially Kean was technically not a star at Drury Lane, since he was a member of the regular company there. At the Haymarket, however, or the Coburg or the City Theatre in the east of London, where Kean made special appearances at one time or another, he was considered a star.[59] It was the spread of the 'star system' itself that extended the meaning of the term to include the central attraction on his or her own ground. A comment of 1832 on the rising popularity and success of the minor theatres points out that 'there is at this moment scarcely a minor theatre in London that does not possess one or more *stars*, persons of established celebrity either, or of rapidly rising reputation [*sic*]'.[60]

The phenomena of movable and fixed stars, then, together resulted in an ever more significant decline in the acting company's traditional reputation for balanced ensemble. 'It has been the ruin of the theatres, and the ruin of the drama,' W. T. Moncrieff lamented.[61] Whatever its effects, the star system could not have become so pervasive, over the course of the century, unless a shift in cultural attitudes towards the theatre had not been taking place at the same time. The rise of the star actor in this age should be seen against the increasingly dark background of the plight of the theatre. Owing to complex factors, ranging from religious prejudice, economic

[58] Letter dated 13th [October 1822] in Hawkins, III, f. 56.
[59] *Report*, Qq. 1478, 3906.
[60] *Tait's*, November 1832, quoted in Nicholson, p. 307.
[61] *Report*, Q. 3171.

hardship and preoccupation with politics to the advancement of the dinner hour into the evening, the major theatres were losing a sizeable portion of their traditional audience and, at the same time, were at a loss how to deal with a potential new one. The emergence of the star in the early nineteenth century, then, can be viewed in this context as the answer to a manager's prayer for someone, anyone, who might appeal more or less indiscriminately to all who could fill his theatre. Where one segment of the audience preferred old-fashioned tragedy or comedy, another was impressed by pantomimic transformations, melodramatic revelations or dogs and elephants: What Kean possessed—along with, to name only a few others, Siddons, Braham, Munden, Mathews, Macready and the melodramatic actor T. P. Cooke—was an ability to appeal in the most compelling theatrical way to the audience's sense of common humanity.

Built on that foundation, the characterizations of the great actors and actresses of the period grew eminent by virtue of another, contrasting quality, the force of an eccentric or even extreme personality. Whether the character was the wayward, self-pitying Byronic hero of Maturin's *Bertram*, acted by Kean with saturnine aplomb, or Munden's Greenwich sot Old Dozey in Thomas Dibdin's farce *Past Ten O'Clock*, it was a memorable deviation from the familiar figures of everyday life. The conviction of reality fostered by an art of this sort was, consequently, based on a sophisticated analogy drawn in performance between real speech and behaviour and the virtual forms that serve truth in the theatre. The players of Kean's age proceeded—unwittingly, perhaps—on this basis, as did others in other times. But the fact that they were, or became, known as regular members of the repertory company meant that audiences would tend to view them as persons too, not just as more or less anonymous entities completely submerged in character. Lamb's comment on Munden's old men sets the phenomenon in illuminating perspective. Lamb once saw Munden play three separate roles in a single evening, 'but they were so discriminated, that a stranger might have seen them all, and not have dreamed that he was seeing the same actor'.[62] The point is that a stranger would miss the happy resonances Lamb feels from the performance of an actor who is simultaneously part of and separate from each character he plays.

The feeling, obviously, is not simply one for a certain style of playing. It goes deeper than this, ultimately touching on the forces that unite the theatre with surrounding life. For all its faults, the repertory company was extremely effective in making such contact, establishing in the audience a sense of intimacy with the player that survived and continued to flourish even after the phenomenal enlargement of the playhouse early in the age. As both *actors* and *players*, devoted at once to their craft and to their audience's appreciation of it, performers in this tradition developed a sense of the theatre that sometimes even accompanied them into everyday life. Lamb's description of Elliston's personality sums up a pervasive attitude and a comprehensive sense of style:

You had a spirited performance always going on before your eyes, with nothing to pay. As where a monarch takes up his casual abode for a night, the poorest hovel which he honours by his sleeping in it, becomes *ipso facto* for that time a palace; so wherever Elliston walked, sate, or stood still, there was the theatre. He carried about with him his pit, boxes, and galleries, and set up his portable playhouse at corners of streets, and in the market-places. Upon flintiest pavements he trod the boards still; and if his theme chanced to be passionate, the green baize carpet of tragedy spontaneously rose beneath his feet.[63]

[62] 'The Death of Munden', *The Athenaeum*, 11 February 1832, in Lamb, I, 342.

[63] 'Ellistoniana', *Englishman's Magazine*, August 1831, in Lamb, II, 168–169.

CHAPTER FIVE

Plays Old and New: The 1790s

The first instinct of the English repertory theatre is to rely on the tried and proven. Its second instinct is to seek out the new, especially if only slightly different. Both instincts are a matter of sheer survival. A glance through any season of the Reverend John Genest's ten-volume calendar of performances, *Some Account of the English Stage* (Bath, 1832), which chronicles the London theatre from 1660 to 1830, reveals the dominance of the known commodity. 'Never acted', the phrase Genest prefixes to the title of each new play, indicates only a transient novelty. Change comes very slowly under conditions of this kind. Over the forty or so years from 1790 the slow, piecemeal development of the repertoire occurs in the context of a reassuringly familiar dramatic tradition some two centuries old.

The titles of many plays presented at Covent Garden, Drury Lane, and the Haymarket during the 1829–30 season remarkably resemble those from four decades before. Not surprisingly, Shakespeare remains the perennial favourite, with over half of his works in regular evidence, including the same range of comedies, tragedies, histories, and romances familiar to present-day playgoers and readers. Only three other authors from the sixteenth and early seventeenth centuries find a place on the stage of the later period. While a few plays of Fletcher and Jonson survive the real workhorse of the non-

84

Shakespearean repertoire is Massinger's indestructible *A New Way to Pay Old Debts*, whose chief character, Sir Giles Overreach, will continue to fire the ambition of actors and the indignation of audiences for decades to come.[1]

Among the dramas that survived from the Restoration there is an evident preponderance of a genre also exploited by later authors: the pathetic tragedy. The obvious favourites are Otway's *Venice Preserv'd* and Rowe's *Jane Shore* and *The Fair Penitent*, whose central female roles of Belvidera, Jane Shore, and Calista had become the jealously guarded prerogatives of generations of English actresses, most notably Sarah Siddons. Other plays of similar tendency and comparable drawing power include Congreve's sole tragedy, *The Mourning Bride*, Thomas Southerne's *The Fatal Marriage* (later altered by Garrick and acted under the title of its heroine's name, *Isabella*), Otway's *The Orphan*, and Dryden's chastely constructed vehicle for high emotions, *All For Love*. Less than half a dozen comedies supplement the list. Despite subsequent critical esteem for *The Way of the World*, the most familiar of Congreve's comedies to theatre audiences was *Love For Love*. The wit of Wycherley, rendered unlicentious, was not unknown, as indicated by an occasional appearance of *The Plain Dealer* and frequent performance of *The Country Wife*, inoffensive in Garrick's alteration as *The Country Girl*. Two other comedies, lively and charming as any in the period, achieved consistent popularity: Susannah Centlivre's *A Bold Stroke for a Wife* and her *The Wonder; or, A Woman Keeps a Secret*.

Perhaps even better known are the comedies from the eighteenth century that filled out the repertory of the early nineteenth. Gay's immortal comic ballad opera *The Beggar's Opera* stands inevitably at the head of the group. From early in the period comes Farquhar's joyful country comedy of marriage and divorce, *The Beaux' Stratagem*, seconded by his *The Recruiting Officer*; from mid-century, Garrick's collaboration with the elder George Colman on the subject of love and money, *The Clandestine Marriage*; and, from later in the century, Goldsmith's anti-sentimental, 'laughing' comedy *She Stoops*

[1] See Robert Ball, *The Amazing Career of Sir Giles Overreach* (Princeton, 1939).

to Conquer. In a class by himself for sheer frequency of performance is Sheridan, whose opera *The Duenna* and comedies *The Rivals*, *The School for Scandal*, *A Trip to Scarborough*, and *The Critic* (the last commonly played as an afterpiece) kept a range of familiar characterizations before English audiences long after Sheridan himself ceased to influence the theatre of his age. Perhaps the most well-balanced accommodation of sentimentalism occurs in the plays of Sheridan—except for his late melodramatic tragedy *Pizarro*, where feelings conquer continents. Meanwhile Garrick's and Goldsmith's general emphasis on native common sense found a staunch opponent in Richard Cumberland. Self-certified physician to the moral ills of his day, Cumberland followed his most well-known and successful sentimental play *The West Indian* (Drury Lane, 1770–71) and its near contemporary *The Brothers* (Covent Garden, 1769–70) with an entire shelf of works, comic and serious, whose emotional pleas on behalf of outcasts of society and victims of prejudice voice an abiding concern of his period.

Of course, strong social concern had distinguished both comedy and tragedy as early as Rowe and Dryden, who themselves wrote as heirs of an earlier, Cavalier tradition of drama preoccupied with manners and mores. In tragedy this interest was often manifested in plays about women rendered defenceless by natural accident, political intrigue, male hypocrisy or their own (alleged) sexual frailty. Long-lived favourites in this category included John Home's 'Shakespearean' drama *Douglas* (Edinburgh, 1756–57), Arthur Murphy's *The Grecian Daughter* (Drury Lane, 1771–72), Ambrose Philips' *The Distrest Mother* (Drury Lane, 1711–12)—an adaptation of Racine's *Andromaque*—and Aaron Hill's *Zara* (Drury Lane, 1735–36). Still other frequently performed tragedies ranged from the neoclassically decorous *Cato* of Addison (Drury Lane, 1712–13) to plays descriptive of the distractions and perils of contemporary life, such as Edward Moore's *The Gamester* (Drury Lane, 1752–53), whose unlucky hero dies moments before a life-renewing inheritance comes to light, and George Lillo's morality *George Barnwell*

(Drury Lane, 1730–31, originally entitled *The London Merchant*), a plain warning against cupidity to all apprentices, who obligingly filled the theatre for years and years on the twenty-sixth of December to be duly warned.

These were the chief plays from the traditional English theatre that became the heritage of the early nineteenth century. At the close of the eighteenth century, however, came a decade that not only contributed its share to the tradition but itself proved crucial to the development of new drama in years to come. With regard to the patent theatres themselves during this decade the most noticeable change, as we have seen, occurred in their phenomenal physical enlargement. As contemporary observers and later historians were quick to point out, this had inevitable effects on acting styles and on the drama itself, now committed—irrevocably, it seemed—to a sustained appeal to the spectator's eye. More subtle, however, and more profoundly significant, were changes in the generic identities of plays themselves. In this respect the drama of the decade beginning in 1790, interesting in its own right, serves as a true forecast of later conditions.

John O'Keeffe's fast-paced Covent Garden comedy *Wild Oats; or, The Strolling Gentlemen* possesses a certain timeless quality. It might have appeared a quarter-century before or after its opening performance in April 1791 without causing anything other than smiles of recognition. A deft manager of comic intrigue, O'Keeffe spins out the story of young Rover, trained to the stage from infancy, whose letter-perfect knowledge of the stock repertoire enables him to fit a quotation to any situation. Evidently, the playgoer's delight depends on recognizing the sources and contexts of Rover's ranging allusions. The play's enduring popularity, then, speaks eloquently of the vitality of the repertory system and provincial touring and the homogeneity of its audience. And yet *Wild Oats* could not have lasted without O'Keeffe's mastery of equally well-known conventions of eighteenth-century comedy. The relationship between Sir George Thunder, an old sea captain, and the exuberant prodigy Rover, who turn out to be father and son, is based on the same premise that

87

Goldsmith, Sheridan, and Cumberland were content to accept: society's ultimate approval of honest hearts and open minds.

An even more familiar title, and a staple of the repertoire for years to come, is Thomas Holcroft's *The Road to Ruin*, first acted at Covent Garden on 18 February 1792. Holcroft's brilliant use of convention illuminates the real liveliness of the play, a sprightly piece in the vein of English comedy of manners. Young Harry Dornton is a big spender, an archetypically prodigal son, but his heart is in the right place and brimful of filial love. Old Dornton, a wealthy merchant, alternately despairs ('Who would be a father?') and exults ('Who would not be a father?'), depending on Harry's latest departure from or return to sense.[2] The main action concerns Harry's extravagance and the calamitous consequences, so great that at the crisis of the play Old Dornton's trade is poised on the verge of ruin. Realizing this, Harry offers to sell himself in marriage to the Widow Warren, who to satisfy her own libidinous desires has thwarted her daughter's romantic hopes and left her deceased husband's natural son to rot in debtor's prison. Meanwhile a moneylender called Silky has obtained the husband's will stipulating that on remarrying she forfeits her inheritance. He offers to sell it for one-third the principal to the Widow and Goldfinch, a speculative son of the turf who would be happy to marry her and live on the remainder (Plate 8). Fortunately, a timely stroke of financial luck frees Harry from his onerous resolution. Old Dornton regains solvency, Goldfinch and the Widow are exposed, and Harry will marry her patient (and quite colourless) daughter Sophia.

Set securely in a structure derived from Restoration comedy and dependent on a similar display of characterization, *The Road to Ruin* appears a sort of sentimental *Way of the World*. Harry, like Mirabel before him, is willing to make love and promises to a repulsive old woman, but between him and his predecessor lie the tender conscience of Steele's Bevil Junior and the ultimate generosity of Sheridan's Charles Surface. Similarly, Goldfinch is the not-so-remote descendant of the Restoration fop, in place of whose lace-edged and perfumed

88   [2] *The Road to Ruin* (1792).

excesses Holcroft has substituted a passion for horse-racing and a recurrent involuntary expression—'That's your sort!'—that identifies one of the numerous progeny of the Jonsonian humours character.[3] The play, then, ingeniously updates vigorous elements of traditional English comedy, including the deft unfolding of character within a skilfully managed complex action. In addition, Holcroft set in motion a new tendency, as Hazlitt explained in describing *The Road to Ruin* as a type of comedy 'in which the *slang* phrases of jockey-noblemen and the humours of the four-in-hand club are blended with the romantic sentiments of distressed damsels and philosophic waiting-maids, and in which he has been imitated by the most successful of our living writers'.[4] More generally described, Holcroft's play shows the impress of forces even then beginning to exert themselves on the plays of the period: a preference for hybrid generic forms and, at least intermittently, a fascination for moral reflection.

No greater contemporary exponent of this latter tendency existed than Richard Cumberland, whose drama *The Jew* was produced at Drury Lane in May of 1794. As the *Morning Chronicle* put it in summarizing the playwright's contribution, Shakespeare's character of Shylock had transmitted a powerful prejudice that had left his entire tribe 'under an impression of odium and detestation almost insurmountable'. All the more to Cumberland's credit, then, the reviewer concluded, is the title role of Sheva, who reveals 'such benevolence of heart, such rectitude of principle, and such correct consonancy of human character' that he matches the authority of Shakespeare's portrait.[5] Fulsome praise, no doubt, but of a piece with the reputation Cumberland long enjoyed for persuasive sympathetic characterization. In 1814, when Kemble had once again performed the role of Penruddock in *The Wheel of Fortune*

[3] Nearer at hand, a precedent for Goldfinch lies in the character of Squire Groom in Macklin's *Love à la Mode* (Drury Lane, 1759–60); see the review of *Road to Ruin* in the *Monthly Review*, 7 (1792), p. 334.

[4] 'On the Comic Writers of the Last Century', *The English Comic Writers*, in Hazlitt, VI, 166. Hazlitt may perhaps have in mind W. T. Moncrieff, author of the low-life burletta *Tom and Jerry*.

[5] 30 May 1794.

(Plate 9), written for him by Cumberland and first exhibited at Drury Lane in February 1795, *The Times* critic described the playwright's forte in familiar terms. This 'species of tragedy character', he observed, 'affords little or nothing of bursts and flights: but exhibits coolness, reflexion, subjugation of temper and passions; a distaste for the pleasures and business of the world, mixed and beautified by a warm, sincere, and active spirit of benevolence'.[6] Keenly responsive to the pressures of his age, Cumberland had found himself repeatedly drawn to create a single, central characterization whose chief interest lies in an inflexibly consistent emotional posture. This character's mental attitude, one of graceful tolerance or melancholy forbearance in a hostile world, carried over from the early comedies into later more serious plays and melodramas.

In this respect the romantic tragedies of early nineteenth-century writers like Sheil, Maturin, Milman and Knowles owe a good deal to Cumberland's example. But this is not to say that sound dramatic action and swiftly paced intrigue were somehow falling into disuse. On the contrary, extensive structural experiments took place in this period of the 1790s. At the Haymarket the younger George Colman was developing a fresh, unorthodox mixture of dramatic kinds that looked directly towards melodrama. Meanwhile, at Covent Garden, Thomas Morton's first play *Columbus*, acted in November 1792, revealed a bold new hand at work on currently fashionable materials.

Although Morton's *Columbus; or, A World Discovered* remained in the regular repertoire for only three seasons, the play evinces the author's remarkably keen sense of what might please and amuse an English audience. Morton competently manages, not two actions, but three. The first is a framing device, orienting the subject matter and providing a neat outcome at the end. Columbus discovers America, but when he shows a benevolent concern for the natives he is overthrown by his villainous officer, Roldan, wrapped in chains, and set adrift in a leaky boat. Miraculously, he turns up with Spanish

[6] 2 November 1814.

reinforcements at the conclusion of the play and puts down Roldan's mutiny.

Within this framework two related actions, one serious, the other comic, develop. Borrowing a pathetic tale from Marmontel's popular romance *Les Incas*, Morton dramatizes the love of the young Spaniard Alonzo for Cora, a native girl who has pledged herself a perpetual Virgin of the Sun. The penalty for tampering with her vow, or person, is death, but in an earthquake Alonzo rescues Cora by sweeping her up in his arms. They are observed; Cora is condemned to die and Alonzo urged to flee. He refuses and, as Cora is about to be put to death, once again rushes in and saves her. Timely news of Columbus's return establishes Spanish authority, and Alonzo and Cora live in happy reprieve. In contrast, the comic action has for its chief character Harry Herbert, the son of an English yeoman (than whom an honester man ne'er lived) who joins Columbus's expedition to the New World and falls in love with a native girl, Nolti. In several scenes we see them banter over love while two buffoons try unsuccessfully to steal her away. Harry, obviously a device for shaping the audience's attitudes, is the archetypal British tar, redolent of salt spray, courageous, honest, reassuringly familiar. Principal source of the comedy interpolated into the serious plot, he embodies the virtues of patriotism and plain dealing that enable spectators to congratulate themselves, while they are laughing, for being English.

The plan, then, is based on a structural principle of alternation, and the individual scene is built to an easily felt climax, yielding amusement in the comic segments and pathos or terror in the serious. No scene is very long, and even this relatively brief text is occasionally marked with inverted commas, the invariable indication of dialogue omitted in performance.[7] Clearly, any hint of over-expansiveness— definable as unproductive repetition of the same emotion— must be excised. Motivations are simple: Columbus is an unswerving man of high heroic virtue, a seafaring Almanzor; Roldan a mere dastardly villain and a coward as well, when the chips are down; Cora a sweet, tearful maiden in distress,

---

[7] *Columbus; or, A World Discovered. An Historical Play* (1792).

dutiful to her father but troubled by the force of love at first sight for Alonzo. Alonzo himself, strictly speaking the second hero of the play, is in effect its first, since Columbus appears only initially and at the end. Bearer of the happy burden of heroic interest, Alonzo has a natural affinity for the pathetic that consistently sets the tone of the scenes in which he appears.

The title page of *Columbus* proclaims it simply 'An Historical Play', but in fact it possesses unmistakable qualities of melodrama and succeeds with them before an English audience a full decade prior to the emergence in 1802 of the first English melodrama labelled as such, Holcroft's *A Tale of Mystery*. High in importance to this genre is the presence of a character who embodies values and principles with which an audience may sympathize or even identify, in this case Harry Herbert. Although he shares a full-fledged nautical identity with his ancestor Ben, the carefree sailor in *Love For Love*, Ben remains an uncouth curiosity in Congreve's correct society, whereas Harry is not only pivotal to the action of Morton's play but the key to its ethos. He is, in effect, a stage surrogate for the audience. No surer sign exists in the drama of the period of the forces exerted by a new age, to which playwrights like Morton were unerringly, if sometimes unwittingly, responding.

That response is evident again in a later work of Morton's, produced at Covent Garden in February of 1800. *Speed the Plough* is no doubt his most well-known play, memorable partly for his invention of a universal symbol for iron propriety of thought and deed, the character of Mrs. Grundy—who, appropriately, never appears on stage. The audience surrogate in this play is Farmer Ashfield, who, not exactly instrumental to the action, nevertheless functions as the structural centre of the play, being the point of contact between two disparate plots. The values implicit in Morton's ordering of his material provide an interesting commentary on the English theatre's ability to assimilate the strikingly new within familiar convention. In *Speed the Plough* Morton combines the paternity plot of late eighteenth-century Gothic drama with a comedy about the solid English yeomanry, so importing the extravagantly romantic subject matter of traduced elder brothers and obscurely raised illegitimate offspring into the sunny realm of common country life, whose centre is Ashford's simple cottage and his own stalwart bearing as a character. When Ashford's adopted son Henry wins a ploughing contest, the young man asserts values undoubtedly nurtured by his foster parent: 'It is the first honour I have earned, and it is no mean one; for it assigns me the first rank among the sons of industry! This is my claim to the sweet rewards of honest labour! This will give me competence, nay more, enable me to despise your tyranny!'[8]

Henry's defiant speech is aimed at Sir Philip Blandford, the guilt-ridden Gothic protagonist who for mysterious reasons has forbidden Henry to come into his sight. Morton affirms that life's primary values are indigenous in the solid countryman. Yet at the same time he awards an aristocratic identity to his hero, Henry, the illegitimate son of Sir Philip's younger brother, by revealing Henry's true father, the now repentant seducer, years before, of Sir Philip's bride—a brother whom Sir Philip thought he had vengefully murdered. Clearly, Morton and, we must presume, a large portion of his audience need to have things both ways. Henry's aristocratic birth secures his ultimate status, but in assuming it he does not abandon the ethos of the common (English) man. That ethos is reasserted in the comic plot, in which young Bob Handy, torn between a legal union of convenience with the rich Miss Blandford or an undowered marriage of love with Farmer Ashfield's daughter Susan, chooses the latter.

In the large context of the repertory of the 1790s, the plays of Morton and such contemporaries as Holcroft and the witty Elizabeth Inchbald can hardly be termed radical experiments. Yet their works are marked by an overall attempt to come to terms with a freshly emerging consciousness of the way people think and behave under stress. In doing so, they consistently adapt familiar, in some cases even hackneyed, dramatic conventions to new uses or infuse them with new sympathies.

---

[8] *Speed the Plough*, 4th edn. (1800), p. 49.

In this respect no playwright of the period is more typical or important than the younger George Colman, who assumed the management of the Haymarket from his father in the summer of 1789.[9] Although Colman had already broken into the ranks of dramatic authors by way of comic opera and comedy and continued in this vein for the length of his career, he first came to notice in 1787 as the author of what came to be taken as an anti-slavery play, *Inkle and Yarico*. The fact remains that the work is cast in the lightweight metal of English comic opera, having a good solid plot interspersed with songs, including many ballads. Colman's career from this point has been interpreted as a process in which his integrity as a writer and early aspirations to serious themes were undermined by a less-than-intelligent public's demand for action and emotion, not dialogue and meaning, and their preference for novelty in disguise over true originality.[10] To be sure, the harshness of the realities faced by dramatists in this new age is not to be underrated. All the same it is arguable conversely that Colman was attempting to expand the familiar formal limits of popular entertainment to include less easily digested material. What is unusual is not that the forms of comic opera and comedy imposed restrictions on Colman's thematic inventiveness but that he was able, over the course of a mere few years, to induce into them a flexibility undreamt of either by earlier practitioners like the elder Colman, David Garrick, and John Burgoyne or by rigid purists like the irascible critic John Genest, who after the fact dismissed Colman's most ambitious play, *The Surrender of Calais*, as 'a jumble of Tragedy, Comedy and Opera, with a ridiculous attempt at obsolete language'.[11]

The Battle of Hexham, produced in the August of Colman's first year of management, defined the mode in which he evidently intended to work. It remains a moot question whether the musical elements of comic opera have been imposed on the more familiar form of the historical play or

---

[9] Jeremy F. Bagster-Collins, *George Colman The Younger 1762–1836* (New York, 1946), p. 45.

[10] Gary J. Scrimgeour, 'Drama and the Theatre in the Early Nineteenth Century', Diss. Princeton, 1968, p. 68.   [11] Genest, VII, 40.

whether a historical subject has been accommodated within the comic opera convention. Not a piece of seamless craftsmanship, the play contains musical or 'operatic' segments quite separable from the historical action itself, which takes place during the Wars of the Roses. Colman might be accused, but only unfairly, of seeking a Shakespearean precedent. The central characters are his invention, the action details the uncertainties of their private lives, and the play is infused with elements of Schilleresque *Sturm und Drang* tragedy. When Gondibert leaves home suddenly, his wife Adeline goes in search of him, disguised as a man and accompanied by a comical servant, Gregory. Approaching the battleground of Hexham after the Lancastrian defeat, they are captured by a robber band. Meanwhile Gondibert, who has become the robber captain—'One of those / Who, stript of all, by an oppressing world, / Now make reprisals'[12]—attempts to rob the escaping Queen Margaret and her son the Prince. Learning their identities, however, he at once offers help and finds shelter for them nearby. Returning to his stronghold, he meets Adeline. She recognizes her husband, tests him with the story of her hardships, and when he proves still faithful reveals herself. The play ends with assistance given to Queen Margaret on her way to rejoin her forces.

There is coherence in this action, but the more comprehensive unity of the play would seem to lie in its orientation towards the pleasure and entertainment of the audience. There is something for everyone in *The Battle of Hexham*: low comedy and humour, romance and pathos, patriotic sentiment, ballads, songs and choruses. This range of varied entertainment is of course not generated by the nature of the action itself; it results from the elasticity of the form as Colman conceives of it.

By the time Colman brought out his best play, *The Surrender of Calais*, in July 1791, the elements of this form had fully coalesced. A well-constructed work of undoubted theatrical effectiveness, its leisurely pace does not prevent the steady building of interest to a crisis. After a year's siege, Calais is

---

[12] *The Battle of Hexham* (Dublin, 1790), p. 33.

almost starved out by the persistent English and must surrender. In return for a general amnesty, the English King, Edward III, requires six good citizens to come out and be hanged. The six brave Frenchmen who volunteer include the Count Ribaumont, who is not a citizen but a brave aristocratic warrior. His beloved Julia in male disguise exposes the Count before the King and offers herself instead. Edward angrily condemns them both, but the Count in turn exposes Julia—whereupon the King relents and, because she is a woman, releases her. Then, in an even more climactic peripeteia, he gives in to the pleas of his Queen, Philippa, and sets all six citizens free, to general rejoicing.

Brief summary does not really do justice to Colman, whose hand is very sure in all this. It is evidently no strain to combine a strong line of action leading apparently to death with scenes of humour, pathos, comedy and romantic love, interspersed with competent songs and heightened by the thrilling patriotic speeches and true sentiments of old Eustache de St. Pierre, played with great warmth by Bensley. The formula, then, is simply that of variety accumulating gradually, parts attaching to parts, until the whole channels into a single climax effected by the transformation of seemingly inevitable disaster into general happiness. Sympathies are skilfully managed, and the historic setting distances the action sufficiently so that contemporary English-French animosity does not prevent appreciating qualities of individual heroism among the French. At the same time, the distressingly cruel threat of the English king is deftly turned, when he relents, into a demonstration of how the English can outdo the French in honour and generosity.

Although in some of his later plays—*The Iron Chest* (Haymarket, 1796) is a good example—Colman found his materials too complex to do them full theatrical justice, at his best he had a talent like Beaumont and Fletcher's for engaging an audience's sympathetic interest.[13] On the stage of the

[13] See Peter Thomson's assessment in 'The Early Career of George Colman the Younger', in *Essays on Nineteenth Century British Theatre*, ed. Kenneth Richards and Peter Thomson (1971), pp. 67–82.

Haymarket, as on that of the earlier Blackfriars, danger could be of more compelling interest than death. Although Colman's plays are as a whole more sophisticated in technique and, sometimes, in language than many of the melodramas that soon grew up alongside them, they share with that newer mode a fundamental orientation towards the theatregoer's pleasure and surprise. When the playwright has defined his form and tacitly promised never to exceed its limits, the audience is free to accept in comfortable certainty whatever his ingenuity can devise. It seems almost anticlimactic that, before the decade was out, Colman himself had written two full-fledged specimens of melodrama, *Blue-Beard; or, Female Curiosity* (1797–98) and *Feudal Times; or, The Banquet-Gallery* (1798–99).

The period of the 1790s, then, saw the emergence of not a few plays which, in form and spirit, are very close to being melodramas themselves, as well as some that in fact constitute early examples of the genre. The complexity of the period, however, from a dramatic point of view, is unusually great. To describe it accurately, an account must be given of still another phenomenon, important to view in the perspective of early nineteenth-century developments: the Gothic drama.

Late eighteenth-century Gothic should be seen as a pervasive cultural tendency, not exclusively as a literary or theatrical genre. All the same, the popularity of Gothic drama itself and the clarity of the form justify separate attention, especially for the extent to which the genre orients the theatrical production of the entire period. Gothic drama goes back to such earlier plays as John Home's romantic tragedy *Douglas* and Horace Walpole's unproduced drama of fateful family relationships, *The Mysterious Mother* (1768).[14] In the late 1790s this history culminates in the dramatic productions of Matthew Gregory ('Monk') Lewis, better known in his own time as author of the romantic Gothic melodrama *The Castle Spectre* (Covent Garden, 14 December 1797) than for the novel that earned him his sobriquet, *The Monk*, published several years before. *The Castle Spectre*, which became the rage of

[14] See Bertrand Evans, *Gothic Drama from Walpole to Shelley* (Berkeley and Los Angeles, 1947).

London for forty-seven performances that season[15] and long remained a favourite, epitomizes the genre and holds the added interest of boldly augmenting the stock of Gothic theatrical atmospherics. More important, Lewis's play was instrumental in developing the sympathetic qualities of the dramatic villain, and at the same time it achieved an almost complete expression of those dramatic and theatrical elements that would coalesce under the explicit term of *melo-drame* five years later. In these various ways Lewis made, at a very young age, some original contributions to the popular drama of his day despite the self-acknowledged derivativeness of his works. Meanwhile, his career as a whole would eventually illustrate the divisive forces operating in the contemporary theatre and, consequently, the extreme tactics playwrights were constrained to adopt as the price of survival.

The dramatic situation in *The Castle Spectre* depends on the events of a period sixteen years before, when Osmond, the saturnine earl of Conway Castle, murdered (or so he thought) his elder brother Reginald and Reginald's wife Evelina, and so acquired his title. Unknown to him, however, Osmond's scheming henchman Kenric found Reginald still alive, nursed him back to ill health, and imprisoned him in the depths of the castle. As the play begins, Osmond has confined his lovely young ward Angela in order to marry her, seeking in her arms forgetfulness of his crime. Meanwhile her lover, Percy, Earl of Northumberland, plans to rescue her by penetrating Osmond's fortress. The situation, then, is classically Gothic: in a wild, inhospitable setting a hidden event of years past exerts a fateful influence on the present, so allowing an evil force to hold sway over unprotected innocence. In terms of dramatic structure, a simple three-part action articulates the heroine's progress: separated from the hero, threatened by the villain's designs on her chastity or her life, and finally saved from him and reunited with her lover. Countless variations could be, and were, introduced into this structure without altering its basic pattern, evidently a deeply satisfying one to theatre audiences. As long as the villain remained purposively evil, the heroine

[15] Genest, VI, 332.

chaste and defenceless, and the hero temporarily impotent, the pattern worked. Of special interest in the development of the genre, however, is the authorial tendency to write against the grain of conventional characterizations. Although the hero consistently remains powerless until the last, the heroine is sometimes allowed to take matters into her own hands, as Lewis's Angela does in stabbing Osmond to death, in the final scene in Reginald's dungeon, so saving the life of the man who is in fact her father. A more extensive change occurs in the villain. In earlier plays he is *sui generis*; 'determined to prove a villain', like Shakespeare's Richard the Third, he regularly does so by committing a murder or seducing a woman or usurping a title—sometimes all three—long before the action of the play begins. In later, more complex characterizations, such deeds become less than definitive of the man, and his true nature appears only through remorse for his crime.

Lewis brings this tendency out in the open with his delineation of Osmond, who, entering with arms folded and eyes downcast, immediately bares his heart in soliloquy:

I will not sacrifice my happiness to hers! For sixteen long years have I thirsted; and now when the cup of joy again stands full before me, shall I dash it from my lip? No, Angela, you ask of me too much. Since the moment when I pierced her heart, deprived of whom life became odious; since my soul was stained with his blood who loved me, with hers whom I loved, no form has been grateful to my eye, no voice spoken pleasure to my soul, save Angela's, save only Angela's! Doting upon one whom death has long clasped in his arms; tortured by desires which I never hoped to satisfy, many a mournful year has my heart known no throb but of anguish, no guest but remorse at committing a fruitless crime.[16]

The villain's anguished remorse has become the measure of his humanity. This villain emerged in the drama of the second decade of the nineteenth century as the Byronic hero—Byron's Manfred, Maturin's Bertram—but his prototype is evident as early as Joanna Baillie's *De Monfort* (Drury Lane, 1799–1800). Already a species of villain-hero, his sense of guilt too deep

[16] *The Castle Spectre: A Drama* (1798), pp. 23–24.

and subtle for mere motive to make plain, he populates the more sophisticated blank-verse or high prose dramas that aspire to tragedy on the nineteenth-century patent-theatre stage. Consistently, these characters flaunt the psychic scars of perpetual disappointment, for never do adamant playwrights give them world enough and time to savour the fruits of their illicit exploits. Within the providential universe of Gothic drama, the irony of their doom was obvious to all save themselves.

In still another way *The Castle Spectre* looms at the portals of early nineteenth-century drama. From the beginning, Gothic drama had established the convention of a stronghold, almost always a castle, within which the villain could exercise unfettered power. It is possible to consider this setting, with its winding stairways, sliding panels, draughty halls, damp dungeons, and subterranean torture chambers, as a sort of objectified landscape descriptive of the villain's own mind and, by extension, of the audience's fearful sense of the human origins of evil. No one, except for insensitive comic servants, really felt at home in this forbiddingly mysterious habitat, not even the villain. Commonly he did not leave it alive, while others, like the heroine, the hero, the comic servant, the good old man and the repentant henchman, could escape it only through labyrinthine passages to freedom. Lewis, cocksure of his instinct for lucid, fast-paced intrigue, employs an escape plot of this kind. His greatest relish, however, is evidently for what would stretch out and punctuate the course of this action, and here his innovations raised spectacular sensation to new heights. Lewis did not really invent new Gothic machinery, but he rehabilitated such stale devices as the moving suit of armour, the striking bell, and the secretly sprung sliding portrait, and he employed the phantom figure with unexampled ingenuity.

The scene that made *The Castle Spectre* a runaway success had been done before, but never had it been prepared so carefully nor executed so resourcefully. Throughout several acts, attention is drawn to the ghost that haunts Conway Castle—the spirit, of course, of the murdered Evelina. Its authenticity, however, is rendered doubtful by reasonable or even comic explanations. Then, at the end of Act IV, when Angela, alone in her chamber and afraid, prays to the spirit of her mother for protection, the following sequence occurs:

[The folding-doors unclose, and the Oratory is seen illuminated. In its centre stands a tall female figure, her white and flowing garments spotted with blood; her veil is thrown back, and discovers a pale and melancholy countenance; her eyes are lifted upwards, her arms extended towards heaven, and a large wound appears upon her bosom. Angela sinks upon her knees, with her eyes riveted upon the figure, which for some moments remains motionless. At length the Spectre advances slowly, to a soft and plaintive strain; she stops opposite to Reginald's picture, and gazes upon it in silence. She then turns, approaches Angela, seems to invoke a blessing upon her, points to the picture, and retires to the Oratory. The music ceases. Angela rises with a wild look, and follows the Vision, extending her arms towards it.]

Ang. Stay, lovely spirit!—Oh! stay yet one moment!

[The Spectre waves her hand, as bidding her farewel. Instantly the organ's swell is heard; a full chorus of female voices chaunt 'Jubilate!' a blaze of light flashes through the Oratory, and the folding doors close with a loud noise.]

Ang. Oh! Heaven protect me!—*[She falls motionless on the floor.]*[17]

Mrs. Jordan's biographer James Boaden recalled the effect of the sequence:

The set scene, in this theatre, had an oratory with a perforated door of pure Gothic, over which was a window of rich tracery, and Mrs. Jordan, who played Angela, being on the stage, a brilliant illumination suddenly took place, and the doors of the oratory opened—the light was perfectly celestial, and a majestic and lovely, but melancholy image stood before us; at this moment, in a low but sweet and thrilling harmony, the band played the strain of Jomelli's *Chaconne.* . . . And the figure began slowly to advance; it was the spirit of Angela's mother, Mrs. Powell, in all her beauty, with long sweeping envelopments of muslin attached to the wrist. . . . Mrs. Jordan *cowered* down motionless with terror, and Mrs. Powell bent over her prostrate duty, in maternal benediction: in a few minutes she entered the oratory again, the doors closed, and darkness once more enveloped the heroine and the scene.[18]

[17] Pp. 79–80.   [18] Boaden, *The Life of Mrs. Jordan* (1831), I, 347–348.   101

Although his style reveals something of a tongue-in-cheek attitude, Lewis was honest about his motives. The apparition scene in *The Castle Spectre* is anything but organic to the action, its purpose wholly that of sensational effect, and in a postcript to the first edition Lewis confuted critics by acknowledging his commercial ends. The anachronism of black servants in the play was merely for 'pleasing variety', he explained, 'and could I have produced the same effect by making my heroine blue, blue I should have made her'. That Lewis could have done nothing but 'serious' writing is evident in what is undoubtedly his best play, the blank-verse tragedy *Alfonso, King of Castile,* as competent and interesting as almost any in the romantic genre. Fearing its failure, he published *Alfonso* in self-vindication before the first production at Covent Garden in January 1802. Ironically, it succeeded, but only by virtue of an ending altered after the manager Harris objected that a catastrophe calculated to excite horror was 'unfit for public presentation'.[19]

Lewis's numerous prefaces and afterwords, as well as the plays that kept him popular for a decade to come, underscore the increasing divisiveness between poetic drama and the stage evident in the plays and criticism of the day. Ambition to write for the theatre remained—witness the efforts of the major Romantic poets to compose a viable stage tragedy—but its cost is evident in the elaborate condescension of men of letters to the tastes of allegedly tyrannic audiences.[20] The attempt of certain nineteenth-century playwrights to make traditional poetic tragedy serve the stridently voiced needs of another age parallels an accommodation of another sort by writers of melodrama. Meanwhile, as the eighteenth century drew to a close, the theatrical audience whose pleasure, if not profit, remained the object of attention was already undergoing a metamorphosis into fragmented, sometimes mutually hostile groups.

A final example of a play spawned in this complex

[19] Preface to 1st edn., repr. in *Alfonso, King of Castile*, 2nd edn. (1802), pp. vi–vii.

[20] See Donohue, *Dramatic Character*, pp. 157ff.

environment may help to place the issues in perspective. The last major dramatic work by Richard Brinsley Sheridan was not his burlesque *The Critic* (Drury Lane, 1779–80) but the grand romantic tragedy *Pizarro*, produced some twenty years later (24 May 1799). Even more notorious than *The Stranger*, introduced at Drury Lane the season before, *Pizarro* was the most successful and financially profitable English adaptation of the work of August von Kotzebue, the prolific German playwright whose romantic and domestic themes, gripping pathetic situations, and unorthodox moral viewpoints created a vogue unparalleled since the days of *The Beggar's Opera*. Although his plays had a wide influence on readers, on the stage the vogue was short-lived; but Sheridan caught it at its peak.[21] Kotzebue was most palatable in the English theatre in plays that clothed a controversial moral issue in the flowing garb of pathos. In addition, it was increasingly evident that Sheridan's theatre best succeeded in heightening dramatic interest by means of spectacle. In Kotzebue's *Die Spanier in Peru oder Rollas Tod* Sheridan found a potentially perfect combination of scenic and pathetic elements in a subject that, he sensed, would also fan the flames of patriotism in English breasts.[22]

That *Pizarro* did nothing positive for Sheridan's permanent reputation as a dramatist is quite beside the point in the context of the contemporary theatrical situation, where the play served admirably to rescue the troubled fortunes of the Drury Lane treasury. Sheridan's flattery of his audience's belief in its own appreciation of high art was never more cunning, in his years as manager, than in the instance of his own last play. Scrutiny of *Pizarro* nevertheless yields immediate evidence, to modern eyes, that the conventions and characters of melodrama have been pressed into service under the spurious colours of pseudo-tragedy. The death of the Peruvian hero, Rolla, played by Kemble with consummate single-minded bravado, is a senseless loss, unqualifiedly pathetic, resulting neither in insight nor in resignation. Even to consider that it

---

[21] Nicoll, III, 64–69.
[22] For a detailed analysis of the play see Donohue, *Dramatic Character*, pp. 125–156.

might have had such an effect is to misread the evidence; Sheridan's aim was utterly different. Each age creates its own tragedy, it has been said. Labels aside, the most ponderous consideration, certainly the most difficult, regarding the theatre of any age is the question of what constitutes true dramatic vitality. To that question the age of Sheridan, which in effect had already become the age of Kean, had begun to offer some fresh, and profoundly unsettling, answers.

CHAPTER SIX

The Plays of the Early Nineteenth Century: *The Rise of Melodrama*

'Kings are no longer Destinies', Edward Bulwer observed in 1833 in his book *England and the English*. As subjects for drama they arouse only 'irreverent apathy', he explained, and the playwright must consequently turn elsewhere: 'Whither?—to the People! Among the people, then, must the tragic author invoke the genius of Modern Tragedy, and learn its springs.'[1]

Pertinent yet after the fact, Bulwer's advice suggests the complexity of the period in which he wrote. For over a quarter-century English dramatists had been turning, if obliquely, to 'the People'. Moreover, in recent years they had been writing exactly what Bulwer described as 'tales of a household nature, that find their echo in the hearts of the people—the materials of the village tragedy, awakening an interest common to us all; intense yet homely, actual—

---

[1] *England and the English*, ed. Standish Meacham (Chicago, 1970), p. 310.

earnest—the pathos and passion of every-day life'.[2] Playwrights were seldom aware, however, that their subjects suited as high a mode as tragedy, and some would have greeted the suggestion with indifference or downright scorn. For what Bulwer hoped could become tragedy had persistently emerged as melodrama, to the disappointment or outrage of those who still believed in the validity of a classical English dramatic tradition and looked, in vain, for its restoration on the contemporary stage. In context, Bulwer's own responses as a playwright to the challenge of his age—*The Lady of Lyons*, *Richelieu*, and other rhetorical costume dramas—seem a reactionary if not merely a time-serving strategy, however sincere his own motives may have been.

The period of the early nineteenth century is notorious as a time when the English drama reached its literary nadir. Nevertheless, something exceedingly important was taking place in the drama of this age. To those who measure progress in terms of development in traditional genres it remains an apparently directionless time, unsure of what tragedy or comedy, farce or even opera was or could become, a time of large-scale trial and failure. Yet the early nineteenth century also saw the birth of the most significant dramatic phenomenon of the era, melodrama. Its precedents lie in Elizabethan domestic tragedy and the eighteenth-century English and French bourgeois dramas of Lillo, Diderot, and others; yet it suddenly becomes a formed and definable entity within a scant few years after 1800. Moreover, under its pervasive influence, much other contemporary dramatic production may be perceived to fall within its magnetic field.

The first English play explicitly identified as melodrama serves as a true prototype of the form and its ethos. Thomas Holcroft's *A Tale of Mystery*, billed as 'a New Melo-Drame', was performed at Covent Garden on 13 November 1802.[3] The author closely followed his French source, *Coelina; ou, l'Enfant du Mystère*, by the prolific Guilbert de Pixérécourt, to the extent of imitating its most novel characteristic, the use of

[2] P. 307.

[3] Playbill (Henry E. Huntington Library).

orchestral music as a running accompaniment to the action. His overall aim, Holcroft declared, was 'to fix the attention, rouse the passions, and hold the faculties in anxious and impatient suspense'.[4] In the plot as adapted, Romaldi wants to marry his son to the rich heiress Selina. Her affections lie elsewhere, however, and he encounters an additional impediment in Francisco, a mute who recognizes Romaldi as his own brother and the perpetrator of the cruel attack that left Francisco without a voice. Thwarted in his plan to murder Francisco and rejected by Selina's 'uncle' Bonamo for his suspicious behaviour, Romaldi fabricates a letter denigrating Selina's birth and escapes to the mountains, where, now penitent, he is eventually taken prisoner.

The fundamental ethical pattern of melodrama emerges in the villain's progress. Here, Romaldi moves from vicious design to vengeance to remorse and capture. Meanwhile, the progress of Selina and Francisco is one through danger to the ultimate revelation that they are father and daughter. An excellent example of the basic melodramatic conflict between good and evil, virtue and vice, occurs in the first scene of Act II, in which Selina is to be married to her beloved Stephano. The scene is a picturesque fantasy: '*A beautiful garden and pleasure grounds, with garlands, festoons, love devices and every preparation for a marriage Festival.*' The dancing proceeds, '*gay, comic, and grotesque*' in the manner of the Italian peasantry, but into this timeless land evil suddenly intrudes. The clock strikes ominously. Malvoglio, Romaldi's henchman, enters and delivers the letter about Selina, and this produces a pictorial reaction to his threat: '*The Peasants, alarmed and watching: the whole, during a short pause, forming a picture.*'

The structure of the play as a whole reflects this conflict of absolutes and the playwright's care to dramatize them in visual terms. In the four scenes of the play, interior settings alternate with exteriors. In the interiors ordinary reality is the mode, but the relatively calm surface of the everyday can heighten the threat of evil by showing it at work insidiously and then more boldly, perhaps under cover of darkness, as in the last

[4] 'Advertisement', *A Tale of Mystery, A Melo-drame*, 2nd edn. (1802).

sequence of Act I. Romaldi has ostensibly retired for the night, leaving Francisco alone at a table. Selina enters and *'gently pulls the sleeve of Francisco: he starts; but, seeing her, his countenance expands with pleasure. (Music pauses on a half close.)'* Selina says, in a low voice, 'Dare not to sleep! I will be on the watch! Your life is in danger!'[5] In contrast, the exterior settings are full of elaborate spectacle and swift action. The effect of this alternation would seem to be that issues are raised through dialogue and then brought to a crisis or climax by visual means. The concluding sequence, in which Selina and Francisco generously try to prevent the killing of Romaldi by the archers who have tracked him down, is conducted principally through physical action and music. No dialogue is heard until the very end, when Selina utters a plea for the remorseful villain and Bonamo asks mercy for everyone, as a slow curtain falls.

In the text itself, then, ample evidence occurs of what the playbill describes as 'Speaking, Dancing & Pantomime'. The term 'Melo-Drame' itself, however, refers to the use of music consistently throughout the presentation. Typical of the directions for music are those in the scene where Selina warns Francisco that his life is in danger. At the beginning the stage is *'dark: soft music, but expressing first pain and alarm; then the successive feelings of the scene'.* As Selina exits after her warning, *'(Music continues tremendous.)'* In the course of the play over fifty cues call for music to begin, continue, change or stop. Music of this sort, far from interrupting the action, enhances it and impels it forward, at the same time clarifying or illustrating its basis in emotion. This expressiveness emphasizes the aesthetic mode of melodramatic art itself. 'A Melo-drame occasionally borders upon a Ballet', W. C. Oulton observed in 1818, 'the action, in striking situations, being accompanied and heightened by music.'[6] In the same year the anonymous author of a preface to S. J. Arnold's *The Woodman's Hut* explained that music in melodrama is no more remote from life than are blank verse or rhyme in tragedy. In fact, he said, 'music

[5] Pp. 19–20.
[6] Oulton, *A History of the Theatres of London* (1818), II, 105.

supplies the place of language, and though the expressions of music are not so nicely marked, still in conjunction with action, the purport of the scene is easy to be understood'.[7] The expressive use of music, then, imposes a definite stylization on the action; it is rhythmic, even balletic. Furthermore, music is not a mere adjunct but an organic part of the drama itself.

By the time James Kenney's *The Blind Boy* was performed at Covent Garden in December 1807, this musical convention had become firmly established and its vital function evident. In the first scene, the peasant Oberto discovers that the sightless infant he has generously reared is the heir to the throne. A messenger has left a mysterious packet in his hands, whose contents he opens and reads:

Edmond the son of Stanislaus,—Heir to the Throne of Samartia.—*(Music expressive of his agitation.)* But let me finish. *(endeavours to read.)* There is a mist before my eyes—I can't see a letter—What, my Edmond, my dear boy, my Prince? *(soft Musick.—his eyes fill with tears, he wipes them.)* Come, come, I must be calm. *(Musick.—walks about in great agitation, with hasty strides.)* What! the Prince Rodolph is no longer—Ha! this is no trifling matter. [*Walks about as before.—Musick.*[8]

Music, pantomime and dialogue together establish a unified, coherent effect, an effect first achieved on the English stage in *A Tale of Mystery*. Despite the prior appearance of plays now justifiably described as melodramatic, the use of music on the French model crystallizes the identity of the new genre beyond doubt.

Basic to this identity is a process of objectification that controls the presentation of character and action alike. The moral posture of the character becomes evident immediately on entrance. Moreover, speech and gesture are not 'realistic'; it is not so much a question of verisimilitude, of providing a convincing impression of the surface of life, as one of exteriorization, of making the inward plain. Sometimes, in more complex renderings of character, tension is created when

[7] 'Remarks' on S. J. Arnold, *The Woodman's Hut*, Oxberry edn. (1818).
[8] James Kenney, *The Blind Boy: A Melo-drama, in two acts* (1808), I.i, p. 14.

a villain's speech maintains a veneer of respectability or honesty while gesture and music simultaneously reveal the truth. More often, speech and gesture render underlying states of mind, attitudes, even conditions of absolute guilt or innocence immediately and unambiguously evident. Holcroft's villain Romaldi, for example, seems compulsively bent on self-betrayal and restrains himself with difficulty. Observing Romaldi, the good old man Bonamo has become mistrustful:

Bona. . . . Good night, my lord; I will send your servant: that door leads to your bed-room. Call for whatever you want; the house is at your command.

   [*Exit with looks of suspicion. Music of doubt and terror.*

Rom. What am I to think? How act?—The arm of providence seems raised to strike!—Am I become a coward? shall I betray, rather than defend myself? I am not yet an idiot.

   (Threatening music.)

Enter the Count's Servant, Malvoglio; who observes his Master.[9]

In this sequence, as throughout the play, convincing psychological characterization is irrelevant. Bonamo's looks of suspicion are, by convention, not to be seen by Romaldi. They do, of course, say something about Bonamo himself, but their primary purpose is to establish and heighten the situation, at whose centre is the villain Romaldi, the threat he presents, and his own sense of being threatened. Menace is in the air.

   The tendency of melodrama to exteriorize emotion, to objectify motive and moral stance, to emphasize role at the expense of individuality, is everywhere evident in its characters; but the tendency finds its fullest expression in the action itself, especially in the climactic moments. Although interiors do occur as last scenes of melodramas, the typical setting is an outdoor place, consistently a wild or otherwise hostile environment. In *A Tale of Mystery* we see '*the wild mountainous country called the Nant of Arpennaz; with pines and massy rocks*'. A rude bridge appears at a height, a mill stream

[9] *A Tale of Mystery*, pp. 16–17.

flows by a miller's house, and there is *'a steep ascent by a narrow path to the bridge'*.[10] The closing sequence of *The Blind Boy* takes place on the banks of the Vistula: *'A terrace, under which the water is seen on the other side, high and winding rocks, against which the Vistula dashes with great fury. In the centre a boat.—Night.'*[11] And in Arnold's *The Woodman's Hut* (Drury Lane, 1813–14) an entire forest is on fire as well as a cottage in its midst and a bridge over the river. At the climax the deserving characters *'escape through the flames over the burning bridge, a part of which falls, blazing, into the river. The fugitives remain in safety on the unbroken part of the bridge.'*[12]

Again and again the implication is plain that the natural world presents unlimited possibilities of accident. As in traditional English Gothic drama, the environment is dangerous and fearful, precisely because what can happen to a person has ostensibly nothing to do with moral integrity or merit. And yet ultimate disaster never occurs. Kenney's *The Blind Boy* again provides a pointed example. Elvina, the heroine, hears the blind Edmond call her from the rock on which he is standing, disoriented and about to fall:

Elvina is seen climbing up the rock—at the sight of Edmond, who is just at the edge of the precipice, she stops a moment, and utters a shriek of horror, and exclaims, Edmond! Edmond!   *(Musick.)*
Edmond. Elvina! *(he falls into her arms.)*[13]

When there is never truly any doubt of the outcome, seeming uncertainty can be highly enjoyable, furnishing all the excitement of actual life but eliminating its dire consequences. The basic rhythm of melodrama serves to make plain what is ordinarily hidden or ambiguous; typically, this rhythm is felt through the climactic display of the immanent. As a contemporary observer put it, melodrama 'places characters in striking situations, leaving the situations to tell for

[10] *A Tale of Mystery*, p. 40.
[11] *The Blind Boy*, II.iii, p. 29.
[12] S. J. Arnold, *The Woodman's Hut: A Melo-dramatic Romance* (1814), III, p. 46.
[13] *The Blind Boy*, III.iii, p. 33.

themselves'. . . .[14] The objectification of emotion in character and action, then, suggests the implicit operation of providential forces. In melodrama, character is destiny, but the laws of the form require this destiny to be manifest from the beginning. In this context, the individual role—heroine, hero, villain, good old man, comic servant and so on—becomes the dramatic equivalent of a lucid predestination. Since the moral posture of the characters is initially clear, the play itself is occupied essentially with a series of *events* which will cumulatively and finally demonstrate the justness of these characterizations. The ethical purpose of melodrama is to reorder the material world so that it mirrors inherent truths.

As a result, melodramatic plays are distinguished by strong qualities of fantasy and wish-fulfilment. The poor blind boy is really the Prince of Samartia. Part of the story of how this came to be is told early in Kenney's play, where we discover a peasant with a history—a contradiction in terms, we must suspect, since apparently anyone with a history is more than a peasant. Obscure birth, or upbringing, lends interesting potentiality to the situation and, not incidentally, engages the sympathies of common men with the character in question. (It is of interest to note that *The Blind Boy*, an afterpiece, was preceded at its first performance by Colley Cibber's *The Provoked Husband*, an early eighteenth-century comedy of manners that reflects the values of a well-to-do society. The contrast in orientation of the two plays is striking.) A prominent feature of melodrama, as of English Gothic drama before it, is the narration early in the play of events that happened years before but which, we soon discover, directly affect the present. In *A Tale of Mystery* such a narrative occupies almost four pages of text, but even in the drastically truncated accounts in later plays the operation of a hidden providence is clear. In Dimond's *The Foundling of the Forest* (Haymarket, 1809) the gloomy De Valmont says to Florian, a young man of mysterious parentage, 'I have long since determined to address you with a brief recital of circumstances necessary to your

[14] 'Remarks' on *The Woodman's Hut*.

future decisions in life'.[15] An extremely long, emotionally charged account of De Valmont's own life ensues, and there is no doubt of its bearing on Florian's eventual happiness.

Although these narratives have a specialized purpose, they share qualities of language evident throughout the genre. Most obvious is the contrast between a stiffly formal and a more idiomatic speech, both styles a function of decorum of character. In these plays, faultless standard English is the language of the aristocrat but also of the common man who has risen to prosperity, the country fellow whose origin and destiny are noble, and the heroine, no matter how low her birth. All are irresistibly drawn to polysyllabic diction, and strong emotions only enhance their articulateness. In Kenney's *Ella Rosenberg* (Drury Lane, 1807–8) the villain Mountfort, finding Ella in his power, makes his lustful intentions plain: 'Loveliest of women, the sacrifice you would make, my eternal gratitude shall repay.' Ella indignantly responds, 'Monster! You excite my horror!—leave me—or I must call to my assistance those who will chastise your insolence.' One tends to agree with Mountfort's retort: 'This is too much!'[16] Yet it remains true that descents into the colloquial are beneath the dignity of all except those of humble station.

In another aspect of language, these plays exhibit notable (and often ill-advised) aspirations to the poetic. Two villains waiting in ambush in *The Foundling of the Forest* establish the time of night:

Longueville. Is midnight passed?
Sanguine. Long since—just as we crossed the glen the monastery chime swang heavy with the knell of yesterday.[17]

Dimond's historical melodrama *The Hero of the North* (Drury Lane, 1802–3) abounds in speeches of high poetic prose that flow in iambic rhythms. The hero, Gustavus Vasa, forced to disguise himself as a miner, meditates his return to felicity in

[15] William Dimond, *The Foundling of the Forest* (1809), II.i, p. 35.
[16] James Kenney, *Ella Rosenberg* (1807), p. 11.
[17] *The Foundling of the Forest*, III.iii, p. 61.

113

these words: 'Oh! will the shining moment never arrive, . . . when yet again this arm shall gleam confessed in war, and hurl avenging thunders on the tyrants of my country?'[18] It is perhaps needless to emphasize that the dialogue of melodrama is, if nothing else, totally functional with respect to action, which is to say that it serves purposes only intermittently connected with complex characterization. As in the plays of other modes, or other times, melodramatic dialogue ranges in quality from the wooden to the smoothly competent; rarely, to the inspired. In the hands of the best playwrights of the time—Tobin, Buckstone, a few others—it has the ring of truth. Too often, however, the voice we hear is that of a whole class of characters, such as sailors, farmers, stewards, lords, Frenchmen and Scots, not of a single individual.

In the brief half-decade after the appearance of *A Tale of Mystery* early in 1802, melodrama established itself as a full-fledged theatrical reality. It is important to observe that this phenomenon took place on the stages of the major houses and that, in this early period, these plays are mostly afterpieces. An exception, Dimond's *The Hero of the North* (Drury Lane, 18 February 1803), a mainpiece not billed as melodrama, proves the rule by showing the clear influence of *A Tale of Mystery*, performed at the rival theatre three months before. A Colmanesque 'jumble' of tragedy, opera, and farce, it lacks the technical consistency and tonal coherence of Holcroft's play, yet its use of music to accompany action in three related moments of a single sequence reflects the French practice that Holcroft introduced to English playgoers and, evidently, English playwrights. The first melodrama by the tireless T. J. Dibdin, *Valentine and Orson* (Covent Garden, 2 April 1804), also reflects the influence of the term 'melo-drame' itself and indicates the ease with which dramatists were able to adjust to the conventions of the genre. Billed as 'a Grand Serio-Comick Romantick Melo-Drama, in Two Acts',[19] it develops unerringly

[18] William Dimond, *The Hero of the North, An Historical Play* (1803), II.iv, p. 43.

[19] Playbill for Covent Garden, 2 April 1804 (Henry E. Huntington Library).

into a pantomime complete with a climactic transformation scene. There is no villain, but unquestionable melodramatic qualities appear in the hero, Valentine, a foundling who makes good, and in the music, *'which varies with the Incidents'*. . . .[20] A similar accommodation occurs with Samuel James Arnold's undistinguished musical drama *'Foul Deeds Will Rise'* (Haymarket, 18 July 1804), in which Arnold crassly exploits his background in comic opera. Such interest as the piece excites arises from the writer's notion of how the light afterpiece might be pressed into extended service. *'Foul Deeds'*, despite its tantalizing echo of *Hamlet*, is basically musical farce, but Arnold by way of experiment has added the Gothic conventions of a murder that took place seventeen years before, a suborned henchman now remorseful over a crime, and a villain whose conscience allows him no peace.

Even where many melodramatic conventions have been effectively employed, playwrights take a certain freedom with the genre, bending it to their own uses and omitting or neglecting whatever seems unpromising. William Elliston's *The Venetian Outlaw*, adapted by Elliston himself from Pixérécourt's *L'Homme à Trois Visages* and performed at·his Drury Lane benefit on 26 April 1805, is a genuine specimen of melodrama and yet reveals not a trace of the French use of music. The play has been cited as a prominent example of the ubiquitous influence of English Gothic drama, from which the German dramatist Zschokke's play *Aböllino* derives and in turn forms the source of Pixérécourt's work.[21] Elliston's adaptation could also be cited as one of countless English plays of the nineteenth century whose immediate origins are French. Aside from the representativeness of its pedigree, *The Venetian Outlaw* stands as one of the first examples of historical melodrama to appear in England and comes fully equipped with the accoutrements of the genre: objectified characters, extensive pantomimic acting, spectacle organic to the action of the play, directions for specific emotional responses (*'They all testify those emotions of joy*

---

[20] T. J. Dibdin, *Valentine and Orson, A Romantic Melo-Drame* (1804), I.v, p. 25.
[21] Evans, *Gothic Drama*, pp. 164–165.

or fear, adapted to the feelings of the different parties'),[22] and a climax in external action, featuring a triumphant exposure of a conspiracy just as it is about to succeed. In addition, Vivaldi, the central character, is a striking early example of the cape-and-sword hero, complete with outlandish disguise: 'Vivaldi *enters as Abelino, with a thick black beard, wild curl'd hair of the same colour, a long cloak wrapp'd round him under which is the habit of a free booter—pistols, &c. in his girdle—forming altogether a stern and most terrific appearance.'*[23]Here is a figure to delight any collector of twopenny coloured prints, just as it must have satisfied Elliston's own flair as an actor for extravagant dramatic statement.

By the time *The Venetian Outlaw* appeared, and certainly by the end of the decade, in plays like Dimond's *The Foundling of the Forest*, the genre had become widely accepted, even by conservatives like John Genest, who remarked that Dimond's play was 'degraded from a place in the legitimate drama' only by the six or seven songs introduced into it 'without any good reason'.[24] In subsequent years the noteworthy developments occur not in the genre as a whole but in its subject matter, as the romantic, sometimes historical melodramas of the very early nineteenth century begin to give place to domestic characters, events and settings. In earlier plays the lords and peasants, castles and cottages of remote middle-European countries stood only by analogy for the persons and places of English life. Later, there began to appear figures recognizably the same as their audience in origin and habit of mind. The quintessential subject of melodrama, as of its Gothic parent, had nevertheless been domestic from the beginning. By the 1820s, in such works as W. T. Moncrieff's *The Lear of Private Life* (Royal Coburg, 27 April 1820) and J. B. Buckstone's *Luke the Labourer* (Adelphi, 17 October 1826), the fact of domesticity had become incontrovertible. It seems appropriate, then, that certain earlier plays, such as Arnold's *The Shipwreck* (Drury Lane, 1796–97), were preoccupied with that charming representative of home life abroad, the indefatigable British

[22] R. W. Elliston, *The Venetian Outlaw* (1805), III.i, p. 52.

[23] I.i, p. 13.   [24] Genest, VIII, 150–151.

tar, long before Douglas Jerrold presented him as the serious hero of the most familiar specimen of nautical melodrama, *Black Eyed Susan; or, All in the Downs* (Surrey, 8 June 1829).

Accounts of the development of a genre inescapably deal with a relatively large body of works, but there are plays in the repertory of early English melodrama that repay individual notice. Part of their interest lies in a substantial record of performances documenting their initial stage success. Moreover, these are plays whose unusual competence and generic clarity help to chart the admittedly ragged course of English drama in a period beset by troublesome forces inside and outside the theatre.

On 21 October 1813 Covent Garden brought out one of the first and most successful of Isaac Pocock's many melodramas, *The Miller and His Men.* One of the liveliest achievements of romantic melodrama, it drew audiences for some fifty performances in the course of the first season.[25] Its plot, simple and easy to follow, provides for a spectacular finish, but the more than ordinary interest of the play results from its full range of appropriate yet varied characters and the excitement of its action. A robber named Wolf, once a retainer at the castle of Count Frederick Friberg, is masquerading as Grindoff, a prosperous miller, and using his mill as a base of operations for terrorizing the countryside. His lust for Claudine, the daughter of a penurious cottager, proves his undoing, however, at the hands of Lothair, a poor but heroic young man who succeeds in blowing up the mill, the miller and his men. Pocock's management of the relationship between characters and action is economical and sure. Kelmar, a cottager (the good old man) is victimized by Grindoff and, in an interesting variation, momentarily made to look like the villain of the piece. Claudine, his daughter (the heroine), lusted after by Grindoff, is kidnapped, imprisoned in the robbers' cavern, and rescued by Lothair in the climax of the play. Lothair himself (the hero), a peasant, engages in subterfuge, disguising himself as Spiller, a down-and-out who seeks vengeance on the Count and joins the robber band. The distance between

[25] Genest, VIII, 416.

117

Pocock's play and the combination of anglicized Schiller and native Gothic still noticeably influential on it can be measured in the resourcefulness of Pocock's hero. Despite capture and exposure, he manages to rescue Claudine and at the same time arrange for the climactic destruction of the mill, which lies directly over a large store of powder in the robbers' cavern. Wolf, alias Grindoff (the villain, or first heavy), an unremarkable character, is assisted by Riber, his henchman (the second heavy), who however is killed at the beginning of Act II, leaving the gap that Lothair fills. The agent of Riber's death is Karl (the comic servant), in the employ of Count Friberg. A funny man because of his perpetual hunger and sensitivity to physical discomfort, he is nevertheless quite undaunted by danger and totally dependable in a crisis. In a rudimentary way Karl acts as a redemptive force that paces the play towards its happy conclusion.

These characters retain a certain vitality while remaining unashamedly conventional. The sole approach towards a more complex psychological portrait is Ravina (the female heavy), Grindoff's mistress, a character reminiscent of the miserable fallen woman Elvira, Pizarro's mistress in Sheridan's *Pizarro*. Still emotionally attached to her seducer, Ravina hates what he represents. Her repentance leads her to become an agent of the hero, who dissuades her from poisoning the captive Claudine out of jealousy. Finally, there is Count Frederick Friberg (the second lead). A largely symbolic personage, he stands at the head of a traditionally feudal society in the far-off Bohemia of the play's setting, but he is a passive functionary, noble and rich and therefore ripe for plunder by robber bands. A generation before, he would have been portrayed as the deserving victim of sentimental outlaws who divide their spoils with the poor. Here he is a necessary but colourless authority figure, remaining on the periphery of the action.

The pyrotechnics that bring *The Miller and His Men* to such a spectacular end differ only in degree from other melodramatic finishes. Sensationalism was swiftly becoming an essential ingredient of theatrical effectiveness in both major and minor houses. In contemporary dramatic context, the rescue scene in

1. Theatre Royal Covent Garden of 1808–9, auditorium in 1810

THEATRE ROYAL, DRURY-LANE.

This present WEDNESDAY, January 26, 1814,

Their Majesties' Servants will perform SHAKSPEARE's Play of the

MERCHANT OF VENICE.

Duke of Venice, Mr. R. PHILLIPS,
Antonio, Mr. POWELL,
Bassanio, Mr. RAE,
Salanio, Mr. I. WALLACK, Salarino. Mr. CROOKE,
Gratiano. Mr. WRENCH,
Lorenzo, Mr. PHILIPPS,

With the Songs, " *To keep my Gentle Jessy*," (composed by Dr. ARNE.)
and " *Softly rise, O southern breeze*," (by Dr. BOYCE.)

Shylock, Mr. KEAN, from the Theatre Royal, Exeter,
(*His First Appearance at this Theatre,*)
Launcelot, Mr. OXBERRY,
Tubal, Mr. MADDOCKS, Balthazar. Mr. BUXTON,
Gobbo, Mr. WEWITZER.

Portia, Miss SMITH,
Nerissa, Mrs. HARLOWE,
Jessica, Mrs. BLAND,

With the Song, " *Haste Lorenzo*," (composed by Dr. ARNE.)
In Act III. A Duett, by Mrs. BLAND, *and* Mr. PHILIPPS.
(Composed by Mr. SHAW.)

After which, will be revived (First Time these Nine Years,) MURPHY's Farce of the

APPRENTICE.

Wingate, Mr. GATTIE,
Dick, Mr. BANNISTER,
Gargle, Mr. PENSON,
Simon, Mr. OXBERRY,
Irishman, Mr. FISHER, Scotchman, Mr. CARR,
Porter, Mr. BUXTON, Watchman, Mr. CHATTERLEY,
Spouters, Messrs. EVANS, I. WEST, APPLEBY, &c.
Charlotte, Mrs. ORGER.

VIVANT REX ET REGINA. NO MONEY TO BE RETURNED. [Lowndes and Hobbs, Marquis Court, London.

To-morrow, (10th Time,) the favourite New Opera of NARENSKY, with (26th Time,) the Grand Oriental Spectacle of

ILLUSION:
Or, the TRANCES OF NOURJAHAD,

On Friday, CIBBER's Comedy of SHE WOU'D AND SHE WOU'D NOT, with, (26th Time,) the popular Pantomime of HARLEQUIN HARPER.

On Saturday, The Opera of the DEVIL's BRIDGE. *Count Belino*, Mr. BRAHAM. To which will be added, (27th Time,) the Grand Spectacle of ILLUSION ; *or, the Trances of Nourjahad.*

On Monday, (First time at this Theatre,) The Comedy of WILD OATS, with 27th time,) HARLEQUIN HARPER.

A NEW FARCE
Is in Rehearsal, and will be produced immediately.

The Comick Opera of the SIEGE OF BELGRADE, and the Musical Farce of LOVE In a CAMP; *or, Patrick in Prussia*, are in preparation, and will shortly be revived.

MRS. SIDDONS,

*in the Character of Isabella in
Measure for Measure,
by Shakespere.*

3. Mrs. Siddons as Isabella in *Measure for Measure*

5. 'King John's first appearance at the New Theatre Covent Garden' (George Cruikshank)

7. Edmund Kean as Sir Giles
   Overreach (W. Heath)

6. Edmund Kean as Othello

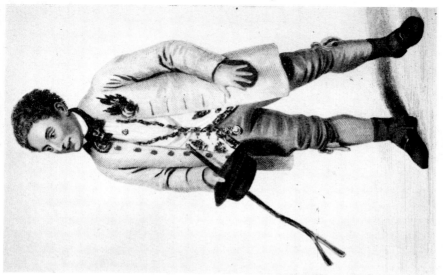

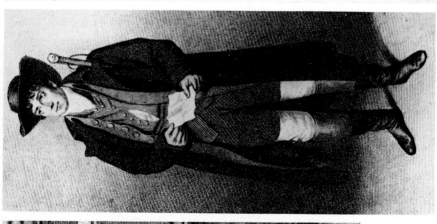

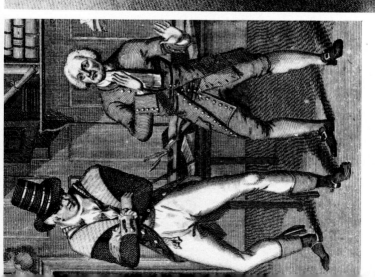

8. Lewis as Goldfinch,
Quick as Silky in *The
Road to Ruin*

9. John Philip Kemble as
Penruddock in *The
Wheel of Fortune*

10. Edward Knight as
Hodge in *Love in a
Village*

12. W. T. Moncrieff

11. J. B. Buckstone

Pocock's dramatization of Scott's novel *Rob Roy* as *Rob Roy Macgregor; or, Auld Lang Syne* (Covent Garden, 1817–18) is remarkable for its restraint. More typical is the final sequence of George Soane's Drury Lane afterpiece *The Innkeeper's Daughter* (1816–17), in which the falsely accused murderer Richard, having been set adrift in a boat that capsizes during a violent storm, almost drowns swimming to a large rock but is then rescued by the fearless heroine Mary.

Soane's play is additionally noteworthy as one of the first melodramas set in England. Based on Robert Southey's metrical ballad 'Mary, the Maid of the Inn', it elaborates a romantic plot involving smugglers and rejects the pathetically sad fall of Southey's character into insanity in favour of her amazingly resourceful rescue of her innocent lover. Such is the stuff of which melodramas are made. Yet, notwithstanding the predictable penchant for rearranging the world to suit the deserts of the virtuous, glimmerings of what must ineluctably be called realism appear in melodrama in the course of the second decade of the century and, more markedly, in the next. H. M. Milner's *The Jew of Lubeck; or, the Heart of a Father*, a two-act afterpiece given at Drury Lane in the 1818–19 season, is set conventionally in distant Europe, but the sustained focus on the psychological distress of its central figure reveals the broadening ability of melodrama to include emotional complexity within the outlines of an established role. Placing such an emphasis on specifically English character, however, may well have struck audiences as a novel departure when W. T. Moncrieff (Plate 12) introduced it in his Coburg melodrama of 27 April 1820, *The Lear of Private Life! or, Father and Daughter*.

The theatrical context of Moncrieff's play requires some attention. When King George the Third died in January of 1820, the patent theatres waited a respectable few months and then within eleven days in April brought out competing revivals of *King Lear* (Shakespeare's play in the traditional acting version by the Restoration adapter Nahum Tate), withheld from the stage for some time in deference to the monarch's incurable insanity. Within three days of the Drury

Lane production on 24 April, Moncrieff's translation of Shakespeare to the realm of domesticity appeared. The subtitle refers to the main source, Mrs. Opie's novel *The Father and Daughter*, but the play's reminiscence of Lear on the heath and its general echo of the relationship of Lear and Cordelia sufficiently justify its title. Seduced by Alvanley and then forsaken after she elopes despite the warnings of her father Fitzallen, Agnes at length turns towards home with her child. In a raging snow storm she encounters her father, who was driven mad by her loss and has temporarily escaped from an asylum. Fitzallen is rescued and allowed to return home, where Agnes restores him to sanity and is reconciled at last with her seducer Alvanley, whose father has died and left him free to marry the object of his true affection. In fleshing out this action Moncrieff alternates scenes of cheerful country parlours, blazing hearths, and songful society with disturbingly pathetic scenes in which his heroine is victimized by hypocrites and abandoned to the elements. The pattern for this technique, established by the younger Colman just before the turn of the century, was described by Charles Dickens forty years later, in *Oliver Twist*, as being like the layers in a side of streaky bacon: 'We behold with throbbing bosoms, the heroine in the grasp of a proud and ruthless baron: . . . a whistle is heard, and we are straightway transported to the great hall of the castle, where a grey-headed seneschal sings a funny chorus. . . .'[26]

It is nevertheless fair to say that Moncrieff dwells on Agnes's plight, and it seems likely that he has adapted the character of Shakespeare's Cordelia to serve as a model of guilt and retribution. In the third scene of Act II Agnes appears in a forest, alone with her infant, at the mercy of the storm; but then her distress becomes agony at the sight of her mad father, dragging a chain behind him and stumbling through the snow, '*dressed in a dark rude suit, his head and neck bare, his beard neglected, his hair matted and dirty, one stocking fallen, exposing his naked leg*'.[27] As Agnes reminds the audience again and again,

[26] *Oliver Twist*, Chap. 17.

[27] Moncrieff, *The Lear of Private Life! or, Father and Daughter, A Domestic Drama*, 2nd edn. (London: Richardson, 1828), II.iii, p. 35.

she herself is the cause of all this. When she later sees her father, still mad, in his cell, she cries out, 'This is the recompense bestowed on him by the daughter he loved and trusted for years of unparalleled fondness and indulgence! Horrible! Horrible!'[28] Moncrieff, like Shakespeare, possessed a craftsman's quick intuition of what would play well. Despite other obvious inequalities it is useful to compare further *The Lear of Private Life* with the play that at least some of the Coburg audience might have been able to call to mind.

Shakespeare begins with a figure apparently locked into his conventional role as king and old man; virtually no hint appears of the humanity that suffering will later elucidate. Fitzallen, Moncrieff's Lear, is in contrast a benevolent old man, the very opposite of inhumane. Consequently his suffering is completely gratuitous. There is nothing in the world that he needs to learn. Aware from the start of the perfidiousness of Agnes's lover Alvanley, he had tried to warn her away from him. For this, ironically, he is visited with great psychological trauma. An anonymous and inscrutable force, unrespectful of human worth, appears to govern human events in Moncrieff's universe. It is not the dark cosmos of Shakespeare's play, however. Because the ways of providence are so obscure, we are shown a senselessly chaotic universe for most of the play, during which time the misfortunes of its unlucky inhabitants give rise merely to pathos. Meanwhile, the intermittent presence of comic elements foreshadows the final restoration of happiness. Perhaps the most profound difference between melodrama and Shakespearean tragedy is that, as in the graveyard scene in *Hamlet*, laughter helps us prepare to accept an ineluctable tragic end, whereas in melodrama laughter reassures us that no tragedy can ever be final. The consistent purpose of the melodramatist is avowed in H. M. Milner's desire 'to produce an entertainment, which, without aspiring to the dignity of tragedy, might yet partake of tragic pathos'. . . .[29]

[28] III.iii, p. 46.
[29] Preface to H. M. Milner, *The Jew of Lubeck; or, the Heart of a Father* (1819).

However much they esteemed the tragic, melodramatic dramatists of Milner and Moncrieff's generation were more concerned with reaching their audiences than uplifting them. In attempting to make contact, they were drawn increasingly to subjects reflective of contemporary life and its problems. Simultaneously, they began to uncover significant limitations in the dramatic form in which they had chosen to work. J. B. Buckstone's *Luke the Labourer; or, The Lost Son*, performed at the Adelphi on 17 October 1826, is surely one of the best melodramas of the age, a piece in which the plotting, smooth and confidently handled, exhibits extensive concern for character (Plate 11). And yet the play reveals the ultimately debilitating influence of the melodramatic genre and its ethos.

Luke, determined to take vengeance on Farmer Wakefield for Wakefield's harsh treatment of him years before, is in league with Squire Chase, lord of the nearby manor, who has designs on Wakefield's daughter Clara. Luke has Wakefield jailed for debt, but Charles Maydew, a prosperous young farmer, donates the needed funds. When the Squire and Luke attempt to kidnap Clara, a sailor named Philip suddenly appears and saves her. Philip pretends to be the messmate of Farmer Wakefield's lost son, carried off as a boy by gypsies (who coincidentally are again in the neighbourhood), and he is welcomed as Clara's rescuer. Then, in the middle of the night, Luke climbs in through Wakefield's bedroom window, bent on murder. But the old gypsy Michael has followed him and makes him discharge his pistol harmlessly. Philip, who has been asleep in Wakefield's bed, leaps up, joins in the struggle, and kills Luke by turning his second pistol on him as it goes off. In the heat of the action Philip suddenly reveals that he is really Wakefield's son, and Michael explains that it was Luke who kidnapped Philip and sold him to the gypsies, from whom he ran away to sea. A joyous reunion ensues.

Buckstone is unusually good at relating character to action, but the greatest interest in the play lies in the thematic conflict between Wakefield and Luke, who has ample reason if not just cause for revenge on his adversary. Originally in Wakefield's service, Luke was dismissed for drinking and unable to find other work. So far the character is that of a conventional villain. But, in addition to making his character the title role, Buckstone gives him a series of speeches that establish genuine claims on our sympathies. Describing the dying moments of his wife, who has perished from starvation, Luke continues:

(*After a pause.*) I were then quite ruined. I felt alone in the world. I stood looking on her white face near an hour, and did not move from the spot an inch; but when I *did* move, it were wi' my fist clench'd in the air, while my tongue, all parch'd and dry, curs'd a curse, and swore that, if I had not my revenge, I wish'd I might fall as still and as dead as she that lay before me.[30]

This is not mere cheap pathos. Moreover, Buckstone has a special design in mind in which Luke's decline parallels Wakefield's, which dates from the loss of his son. What Buckstone has done is to enlarge the limits of conventional character in order to oppose two men, each of whom has suffered at the hand of the other and from misfortunes encountered in the world at large. Regrettably, the idea does not sustain itself to the end. The prior claims of Luke's role as villain too soon overshadow his humanity, and he is sadly allowed to die without achieving even some measure of reconciliation or relief. It is evident what narrow strictures the melodramatic form imposes. Clearly, given the plot of a long-lost son restored, the playwright has felt bound to subordinate more subtle and meaningful human relationships to the task of building a suitably climactic discovery scene. A promise of a new realism emerges from *Luke the Labourer*, but only a promise.

Still, Buckstone at his best is a serious dramatist with a point of view. It is not just that times are hard but that life itself is hard. Uncertainty remains man's perennial lot. It is understandable, we infer, if a man like Luke becomes bitter. When the righteous Charles Maydew upbraids him—'Well, Luke, you need not be so exact'—Luke responds, 'Some folk ha' been exact enough with me, before this time, and now it be

[30] John Baldwin Buckstone, *Luke the Labourer; or, The Lost Son: A Domestic Melodrame* (1826), I.ii, p. 25–26.

my turn; I've had measters to teach me, and I'll show that I've larned my lesson.'[31] Other characters voice what is tantamount to the same view, Dame Wakefield observing, 'Hey, bless me, this is a sad world for the helpless and unfriended!'[32] However ordinary they may sound, these expressions have a thematic force in *Luke the Labourer* that runs counter to the predictable fantasy of the conclusion.

Buckstone was, of course, not alone in following this virtually mechanical compulsion. At the end of the century Oscar Wilde's Miss Prism summarized the ironclad poetic justice that had governed so many authors for so long: 'The good ended happily, and the bad unhappily. That is what Fiction means.'[33] Regardless of their chosen subject matter—romantic, domestic, nautical or, as in later plays, urban—playwrights almost by instinct oriented the dramatic action towards ultimate felicity, achieved not in the next world but in this. Exceptions to the happy ending are few, and startling when they occur; and in the main, pathetic conclusions are reserved for so-called fallen women. From Rowe's *Jane Shore* and 'Monk' Lewis's *Adelgitha* to Victorian melodramas such as *East Lynne,* society's rejection of the female sexual sinner followed the same lachrymose pattern regularly terminating in death and accompanied by the gratuitous forgiveness of husband or lover. In contrast, the woman who preserves her chastity, especially at heavy cost, reaps the rewards of constancy no later than at the end of the last act. Douglas Jerrold's Susan in *Black Eyed Susan* (Surrey, 8 June 1829) is a typically vocal self-defender: 'Take, sir, all that is here; satisfy your avarice—but dare not indulge your malice at the cost of one, who has nothing left in her misery but the sweet consciousness of virtue. [Exit, O.P.'[34] The last-minute reprieve of Susan's condemned husband William becomes in effect a cosmological endorsement of her faithfulness. Rachel, the unjustly accused heroine of Jerrold's *The Rent Day* (Drury

[31] I.i, p. 10.
[32] I.ii, p. 21.
[33] Oscar Wilde, *The Importance of being Earnest* (1899), p. 58.
[34] *Black-Ey'd Susan: A Drama* (1829), I.iii, pp. 19–20.

Lane, 25 January 1832) ultimately fares as well, despite the harrowing threat made by her despairing husband Martin Heywood to abandon her for supposedly having sold her favours to Squire Grantley. In another variation, Mary Maybud, the long-suffering heroine of J. T. Haines's charming nautical melodrama *My Poll and My Partner Joe* (Surrey, 31 August 1835), has resigned herself to a loveless alliance. Having given up hope that her fiancé Harry Hallyard is still alive, and having married his partner Joe Tiller, she is shocked almost into insanity by Harry's belated reappearance. She pays a full debt in mental anguish for having doubted that her lover would turn up alive, but in the end she becomes free to marry him when an accident out of the blue takes the life of the unfortunate Joe Tiller, an innocent sacrificed on the altar of true love by a remorseless playwright.

In short, a consistent relationship develops in melodramatic dramaturgy between the disruption of society and its final restoration to harmony. In traditional comedy this movement from disorder to order enables certain characters, often a young man and woman in love, to learn something about themselves and the world and to accept their place in it. Melodrama, on the contrary, does not move towards eventual enlightenment. The reconciliations it provides are of a hostile or uncertain world to the just deserts of already ideal human beings. The more desperately irretrievable the situation, the more satisfying its climactic reversal. The miraculous recovery, the obscure technicality, the sudden shower of gold (as in Jerrold's *The Rent Day*)—all accident only certifies the nature of a world whose charted course is hidden from our eyes but unswervingly true.

It was the very purity of the genre, and the consequent unmixed clarity of the expectations it induced in audiences, that helped to make melodrama so immensely popular. Evidently, it answered deeply felt needs for reassurance, or for the freer exercise of fantasy, symptomatic of problems common to the age of Kean and to later times as well. The relationship between melodrama and society in this respect remains virtually unexplored. (It seems an especially suitable subject for psychoanalytic criticism.) There seems little doubt,

125

nevertheless, that melodrama may be viewed as an appropriate response to profound social pressures and that it began to die when these pressures altered. Threatened by the development of a new realism in the latter part of the nineteenth century, melodrama proper finally fell before the onslaught of change manifested climactically in World War I—not, however, before it had bequeathed a legacy of craftsmanship and point of view that influenced the medium of film and, on stage and screen, continues to exert its force today.

CHAPTER SEVEN

The Plays of the Early Nineteenth Century: *Tradition and Change*

The fact that melodrama became significant so quickly after its emergence at the beginning of the new century says much about the theatre of the age. As if a temporary vacuum had been created by shifting cultural values and the unequal pressures of political and socio-economic forces, melodrama had rushed in with startling swiftness, drawing other forms along with it and altering their characteristics. The reaction in some quarters was other than favourable. Congreve and Farquhar are seldom acted, Charles Lamb lamented, for the pleasure they afford has been spoiled by 'the exclusive and all devouring drama of common life'.[1] Lamb's specific target is the tendency he observes in audiences to be preoccupied with obtrusive moral considerations, but his remarks imply a large-scale disruption of what was once a stable aesthetic. The presence of a comedy by Cibber and a melodrama by Kenney

[1] 'On the Artificial Comedy of the Last Century', in Lamb, II, 142.

127

on the same Covent Garden bill speaks clearly enough of the divisive situation now the rule. 'It is useless to hope for the success of what is called the regular drama,' Charles Robert Maturin admitted in a letter to Elliston; 'I must learn to adapt myself to the taste of the public.'[2] According to another contemporary, the English fondness for melodrama could be traced even in the popularity of certain Shakespearean plays. *Richard the Third*, *Othello*, and *Macbeth*, being 'the most melo-dramatic', were the most often performed.[3]

It will not do, of course, to describe the various dramatic genres of the period simply in terms of the influence melodrama exerted on them. The disintegration of older, more lucid generic forms and the simultaneous development of the more or less amorphous burletta in the minor theatres are also critically important aspects of the subject. Reading the plays of the period, one nevertheless can hardly avoid the impression that tragedy succeeds best as melodrama and comedy as burletta, and either is more apt to do well with a generous admixture of music, especially song.

To judge by the number of playwrights who attempted it, comedy in the early nineteenth century put up a valiant but losing effort to hold its own. Some of the melodramatists of the time, like Buckstone, Jerrold, Kenney and Moncrieff, wrote comedies as well. Authors of serious regular dramas like Sheridan Knowles also tried their hands at it. As for the comic dramatists who learned the craft in the late eighteenth century, not many had survived. Mrs. Inchbald's last play appeared in 1805. By the end of the first decade Frederick Reynolds had turned his attention exclusively to comic opera, melodrama and pantomime. The four comedies written by Cumberland in the new century made little if any mark. *Speed the Plow* remained in the repertoire, but the only subsequent piece of Morton's to attain wide notice was not a comedy but a spectacular oriental melodrama, *The Slave* (Covent Garden, 1816–17).

[2] Undated letter, *ca.* 1821, in Raymond, *Memoirs of Elliston*, II, 215.
[3] Horace Foote, *A Companion to the Theatres; and a Manual of the British Drama* (1829), p. 111.

Similarly, George Colman, having carefully eyed the trend, expended more effort on operatic farce and melodrama than on comedy. All the same, in addition to a widely popular comic opera with the fetching title *Love Laughs at Locksmiths* (Haymarket, 1803), Colman managed to produce what is perhaps the best, and surely the best known, comedy of the first quarter-century, *John Bull; or, An Englishman's Fire-side*, which opened at Covent Garden on 5 March 1803, played for forty-six performances through the end of the season,[4] and became standard repertory fare. Employing characters and situations long familiar to audiences of sentimental comedy, Colman contrasts a preoccupation with status and wealth on the part of pseudo-fashionable London with the perennially sound values of the English country hearth and home, throwing in for good measure the charm and whimsical generosity of the Irish. Set in Cornish country near Penzance, the play presents the successful effort of the long-lost, recently returned Peregrine to unite his younger brother's son, Frank Rochdale, with the brazier's daughter whom Frank has seduced and then regretfully abandoned in order to comply with his father's demand that he marry Lady Caroline, daughter of the socially prominent Lord Fitz-Balaam. The plot has pronounced romantic inclinations, but Colman skilfully fashions it into a showcase for a varied range of English and Irish comic characters. Dennis Brulgruddery, an extravagant eccentric from 'the oul' sod', newly turned industrious innkeeper, tolerates the oppressiveness of wife and weather and blesses his company with inveterate cheerfulness. Shuffleton, a flashy, debt-ridden Londoner with an eye on the main chance, finds a match in Lady Caroline and her crass opportunism and promptly marries her, meanwhile making an elaborate pretence of friendship for Frank and his gullible, social-climbing father Sir Simon. The most vigorous and memorable character of all is Job Thornberry (one of John Fawcett's prized roles), a crotchety old brazier with a heart of gold and a conscience upright as the day is long. The best scene in the play occurs in Act V, when Job, having lost all patience,

[4] Covent Garden playbills (Henry E. Huntington Library).

storms into the manor house, bribes a contemptibly mercenary servant to admit him to the presence of Sir Simon, who also functions as the local magistrate, and sits himself stubbornly down in the seat of justice, vowing not to move until his daughter's rights are restored by marriage to Sir Simon's son.

The title role of *John Bull*, it need hardly be added, is an invisible character, symbolic of the values embraced by the play and unashamedly declared by Peregrine, its spokesman: 'John Bull exhibits a plain, undecorated dish of solid benevolence.'[5] At the end, Peregrine asserts his prior claim, as elder brother, to Sir Simon's estate only because the latter has neglected 'what no Englishman should neglect—justice and humanity to his inferiors'.[6] Such sentiments veer uncomfortably towards claptrap, but Colman succeeds in imbuing at least some of the characters with a vitality that speaks of actual life more than the stultifying conventionalities of a derivative comic stage.

Shortly after the turn of the century, Thomas Gilliland had described the subject matter of comedy as 'the infinitely various passions and pursuits of mankind in the common transactions of life',[7] but the description exceeds the contemporary reality. If comedy as such had fallen into undeniable decline, however, transmutations of comedy appeared with increasing frequency as the minor theatre burletta began to prosper and the major theatres' instinct for survival encouraged experimentation. The amazingly prolific Dibdins, Charles junior and Thomas John, supplied Sadler's Wells, the Royal Circus, and the Surrey, as well as Covent Garden, with spectacles, pantomimes, operatic farces, burlesques, interludes and extravaganzas, in addition to increasingly frequent melodramas, many of which fell within the ill-defined limits of a licence for burletta. Proper study of the Dibdins' contribution and influence must await the appearance of a documented calendar of the London stage in the early years of this century, together with exhaustive perusal

[5] Colman, *John Bull; or, The Englishman's Fireside* (1805), IV.i, p. 69.
[6] V.ii, p. 98.
[7] Thomas Gilliland, *A Dramatic Synopsis* (1804), p. 40.

of such texts and manuscripts of theirs as survive. Meanwhile, it may be useful to glance briefly at some representative works by another author whose career, as much as any, illustrates the range of possibilities open to dramatists of the day.

Aside from a spectacle entitled *Moscow*, whose text has apparently vanished, W. T. Moncrieff's first essay in dramatic form was a musical farce called *The Diamond Arrow; or, The Postmaster's Wife, and the Mayor's Daughter*, performed at the Olympic in December 1815. Of scant interest in itself, the piece does show that Moncrieff had grasped from the start the way to combine broadly rendered characters in a simple action that allows for both a romantic love interest and comic eccentricity, the whole interspersed with songs and choruses demonstrating the young author's competence as a lyricist. In later years Moncrieff turned increasingly towards melodrama, dividing his work principally among the Coburg, the Adelphi, Sadler's Wells, the Surrey and Drury Lane, but he had already earned a reputation before such serious dramas as *The Lear of Private Life, The Shipwreck of the Medusa* and *The Vampire* began to appear in 1820. His two-act operatic extravaganza *Giovanni in London; or, The Libertine Reclaimed* (Olympic, 26 December 1817) adapted the Don Juan story as a sequel that brings a markedly tamer version of the licentious hero back from hell to London, where after some titillating escapades marriage rescues him from eternal shame. The title role provided Eliza Vestris with one of her most successful 'breeches' parts. In addition to its jolly comic songs, written on the plan of *The Beggar's Opera* as new words sung to familiar melodies, *Giovanni in London* is significant as one of the first pieces of the time to employ the actual city of London for a series of settings.

In a higher class of excellence is another work written by Moncrieff for Elliston's Olympic, *Rochester; or, King Charles the Second's Merry Days* (16 November 1818). Billed as a burletta, the play contains nine songs in all—apparently sufficient music, by this date, to disarm charges of breach of licence. In his Preface to the Richardson edition of 1828, Moncrieff claims with some justice that his was the first original minor theatre piece with 'pretentions to the rank of a regular Drama'.

Although *Rochester* inclines noticeably towards farce, it has the tone and energy of a Farquhar country comedy and some laughable multiple disguises that compare not unfavourably with Restoration and eighteenth-century models. The vigorous, well-sustained characterizations of Wilmot Earl of Rochester and Villiers Duke of Buckingham, together with their vivacious pursuers the Countess of Lovelaugh and Lady Gay, raise the work well above the level of mediocre musical farce. In particular, the role of Rochester as Elliston played it must have helped to make him, in Moncrieff's words, 'completely the spoiled child of the Public'.[8] Even the subordinate characters are unusually well differentiated, from Starvemouse, an old miser, and Amen Squeak, the parish clerk, to Muddle the mayor, a compulsive coiner of malapropisms. Arguably Moncrieff's best play, *Rochester* is great good fun and, in the drab context of contemporary failure to charm the comic muse, a singular achievement.

Conversely, it should be added that Moncrieff did not fulfil the promise implicit in this work, even in his most spectacular success, *Tom and Jerry; or, Life in London*, an operatic extravaganza that presents the adventures of a rustic Somerset fellow, Jerry Hawthorne, and his city cousin Corinthian Tom, who has volunteered to initiate Jerry into the delectable mysteries of London life. Quite unhampered by false modesty, Moncrieff described *Tom and Jerry* as '*The Beggar's Opera* of the present century'.[9] Considering its ballad-opera form, seamy characters and exceedingly great theatrical success, Moncrieff had a point, but the work is utterly innocent of the satiric thrust that orients Gay's earlier masterpiece. Based on Pierce Egan's immensely popular novel *Life in London*, this musical play sets the scenes of London sporting life before its audience with thorough fidelity and populates them with convincingly indigenous characters. All in all, it is exceptionally lively and competent writing. The author evidently knew the patois

[8] Moncrieff, Preface to *Rochester; or, King Charles the Second's Merry Days* (London: Richardson [1828]).

[9] Moncrieff, 'Remarks' on *Tom and Jerry; or, Life in London*, 2nd edn. (London: Richardson [1828]'.

spoken by habituées of the gaming table and the auction hall, and his facility is undeniable, as in Bob Logic's explanation that life in London requires cold cash or, in a word, 'blunt':

Blunt, my dear boy, is—in short what is it not? It's every thing now o'days—to be able to flash the screens—sport the rhino—shew the needful—post the pony—nap the rent—stump the pewter—tip the brads—and down with the dust, is to be at once good, great, handsome, accomplished, and every thing that's desirable—money, money, is your universal good,—only get into Tip Street, Jerry.[10]

Many scenes and briefer moments achieve comparable verve and style. And yet *Tom and Jerry* smacks, however subtly, of the meretricious. Admirable as the sheer competence of Moncrieff's writing is, his plays have a certain sheen that fails to hide a lack of depth and conviction. As a group, they illustrate the price often paid in this age by those who felt drawn, or driven, to earn a living writing for the stage. The price Moncrieff paid was exceptionally high. He ended his days blind, in the Charter-house.[11]

Many of the plays of the early nineteenth century, it is all too true, fall into the gap between aspiration and fulfilment. To be sure, most dramatists seem to have had only modest designs on the pleasure of their audiences and no illusions whatever about their work. Some few, however, entertained loftier aims, hoping perhaps to restore the sovereignty of tragedy or, at least, to find a way to accommodate tragic themes to the capacities and interests of the contemporary public. A handful did succeed, and an account of their achievement serves to describe the real force, although sometimes puerile and ultimately ineffectual, of dramatic conservatism in the theatre of the period.

At the very beginning of the century a highly promising author appeared in the person of Joanna Baillie, whose tragedy *De Monfort*, featuring John Philip Kemble and Sarah Siddons in the leading roles, was produced at Drury Lane on 29 April 1800. This exceedingly ambitious play has an

[10] I.iv, p. 19.
[11] *Dictionary of National Biography.*

estimable importance in the history of the drama despite its sad failure on the stage, for it stands at a critical point between the late eighteenth-century Gothic drama and nineteenth-century innovations in that genre, particularly in the developing psychological complexity of the villain-hero. A few later exemplars of Baillie's several series of 'Plays on the Passions' achieved stage performance, but as a whole they belong, if only by default, with the unacted reading drama of the period. Similar disappointment, on a smaller scale, lay in store for William Godwin. Readers of his often gripping psychological novel *Things As They Are; or, The Adventures of Caleb Williams* (1794) may have sensed excitement at the prospect of his first tragedy, *Antonio; or, The Soldier's Return* (Drury Lane, 13 December 1800). The play does have some genuine interest for the ethical problem it raises, concerning a highly moral man perverted through circumstances into irretrievable error, but its philosophical ideas run at cross purposes with the orientations of dramatic roles, and most of the play is talky and boring. It was withdrawn after a single performance, and Godwin's next attempt, *Faulkener* (Drury Lane, 16 December 1807), lasted for only three nights despite a more interesting intrigue plot, an absence of ethical debate, and a heroine who dies of acute stage tragedy.

Meanwhile, a much more successful play had appeared the season before. On 19 February 1807, Drury Lane brought out John Tobin's *The Curfew*, the best work by a dramatist whose premature death was a loss to the English stage. Even more than its record of twenty performances might have been achieved had not Sheridan mendaciously stopped the run in order to avoid the additional benefit for the author's family agreed on for the twenty-first night.[12] *The Curfew* uncondescendingly takes the Gothic convention on its own terms and reinvigorates it in the process. An index of Tobin's competence lies in his handling of the relationship of hero and villain. The Baron Hugh de Tracy, who apparently committed a murder years before and cannot escape from his conscience, falls into the familiar mould of remorseful villain.

[12] Genest, VIII, 37.

Correlatively, Fitzharding, leader of a robber band whom the Baron once forced to the public marketplace at noon and cruelly branded on the arm for his insolence, is the apparent hero. But Tobin has a surprise in store. In Elliston's earlier *The Venetian Outlaw* Elliston played Vivaldi, who masquerades as a conspiratorial villain but is really the hero, while Barrymore played the true, unequivocal villain Orsano. Similarly, in *The Curfew* Elliston was Fitzharding and Barrymore the Baron. The theatrical context, then, suggests straightforward continuity, but Tobin uses the action of the play to effect a reversal in these adversary roles. And yet it is not the action so much as the characterization that does it. The Baron is an authoritative but fundamentally reasonable man. He accepts the facts of experience, understands that people can change, and respects intelligence wherever it emerges. Fitzharding, whose just grievance against the Baron wins initial sympathy for this leader of Schilleresque woodland robbers, maintains, on the other hand, an inflexible posture of revenge that soon becomes tiresome. A monomaniacal villain to the last, he cries out that he would rather die the Baron's enemy than live on as his friend. The Baron's answer—'He may be wrought on yet'—is an incredible response for anyone, let alone a hero, to make about a villain at the end of a Gothic drama.[13]

In still other ways Tobin makes of the Gothic convention a staff, not a crutch. Employing the device of the resourceful heroine exploited by contemporary dramatists like Lewis, Tobin presents his heroine Florence as intelligent, not just strikingly beautiful. She speaks a forthright, articulate language reminiscent of Shakespeare's heroines, and she has presence of mind, never becoming the object of maudlin pathos even when her life is threatened by Robert, the troubled young man who proves to be her brother. In fact, intelligence is valued wherever it occurs—a refreshing change from plays in which characters are 'fatally' victimized by appearances because they lack inquiring minds and do not look closely enough to penetrate disguises or otherwise come to grips with reality.

[13] Tobin, *The Curfew* (1807), V.iii, p. 60.

The intelligence foremost in evidence is Tobin's own. He manages to make something organic, even thematic, out of a conventional historical setting, England at the time of the Norman conquest, so that the unusual perceptiveness of a few characters stands out against a background of ignorance and superstition. Given the oppressive sameness of Gothic atmospherics, such a treatment of convention may well strike the reader as a feat. Moreover, to Tobin's credit as a craftsman should be added a recognition of his gift as a writer of taut, effective dramatic verse. Tobin had a large and, on balance, well-deserved posthumous reputation for his language. Despite the author's evident enthusiasm for figurative speech, *The Curfew* is not in the least overwritten. Among the few set speeches, none of which impedes the action, perhaps the best is spoken by Matilda, the Baron's long-lost wife, in response to a malicious charge of witchcraft:

> I answer with the voice of innocence,
> That I enjoy the silent hour of night,
> And shun the noisy tumult of the day,
> Prize the pale moon beyond the solar blaze,
> And choose to meditate while others sleep.
> If these are crimes I am most culpable.
> For, from the inmost feeling of my soul,
> I love the awful majesty sublime
> Of Nature in her stillness—To o'erlook,
> Fixt on some bleak and barren promontory,
> The wide interminable waste of waves;
> To gaze upon the star wrought firmament
> Till mine eyes ache with wonder—these are joys
> I gather undisturb'd—The day's delights
> I am proscrib'd. . . .[14]

This is hardly distinguished verse, but it has sinew and a certain clarity and speaks of individual character. As in his comedy *The Honey Moon* (Drury Lane, 1804–5), Tobin's writing is sometimes derivative, usually of Shakespeare, but almost never

[14] IV.i, p. 43.

gratuitously florid. Its serviceability stands out in an age when hardly anyone could write satisfactory verse for the theatre.

For a brief time, however, late in the second decade of the century, something of a revival of blank-verse tragedy seemed at hand. In May of 1816 Charles Robert Maturin, better known as the author of the novel *Melmoth the Wanderer*, succeeded in having his first tragedy, *Bertram; or, The Castle of St. Aldobrand*, performed at Drury Lane. Acted twenty-two times through the end of the season, with Kean in the tailor-made title role, the text went through seven editions before the year was out.[15] Maturin's second work in this vein, *Manuel* (Drury Lane, 8 March 1817), was less well received. Meanwhile, Covent Garden was entertaining ambitions of its own for the Irish dramatist Richard Lalor Sheil, represented there first with *Adelaide* (23 May 1816) and then with three additional tragedies, the last of which, *Evadne; or, The Statue* (10 February 1819) provided Eliza O'Neill with still another grand means of access to her audiences' emotions. And by this time the Reverend Henry Hart Milman, later Dean of St. Paul's, saw his first and only performed tragedy *Fazio* appear on the stage of the same theatre (5 February 1818) after an earlier version based on his edition of 1815 and disclaimed by Milman himself had surfaced as *The Italian Wife* at the Surrey (22 December 1816).

Although one of these plays, *Evadne*, lasted on the stage for some sixty years,[16] their most distinguished general feature is their service as vehicles for actor and actress. It is perhaps understandable that audiences became enamoured of the idiom of these plays because of the high emotions they stirred and the echoes they raised of traditional dramatic art. Extravagantly pseudo-Elizabethan in language, they appear to idealize Shakespearean practice but meanwhile emulate concepts of dramatic character that go back through Restoration pathetic tragedy only so far as the plays of Beaumont and Fletcher and the affective techniques of the Jacobean private

[15] Genest, VIII, 532; Nicoll, IV, 354.

[16] See John Stewart Carter, ed., *The Traitor* (1965), Intro., p. xii. Sheil's *Evadne* is based in part on James Shirley's *The Traitor*.

theatre. [17] Of genuine interest for the student of English dramatic and theatrical development, these plays written in hothouse verse and prose prove keenly disappointing as dramatic literature. Their claim to true conservatism, although uttered in stentorian tones, is specious.

By comparison with these works, a concerted effort at originality shines through the text of James Sheridan Knowles' *Virginius; or, The Liberation of Rome*. The production at Covent Garden on 17 May 1820 brought Knowles instant renown and, not so incidentally, secured the reputation of the actor of the title role, William Charles Macready. Knowles went on to become, at least in retrospect, something of an early Victorian institution, and indeed his first play for London audiences speaks in an eloquent voice of values and ideals that would become quintessentially Victorian. *Virginius* is a high tragedy freshly cast in the mould of an ideal domesticity. The reasons for the play's wide appeal are easy to perceive. Strong emotions are properly clothed in the sophisticated garb of blank verse, so avoiding the roughness of melodramatic minor-theatre prose. Yet they remain uncluttered by intellectual complexity of the sort that made the dramas of Joanna Baillie and Coleridge less viable on the patent theatre stage.

In addition, virtues and principles that remain fleshless in the work of other, more poetically inclined, dramatists find here a concrete basis in the everyday realities of home life. Although the central situation of the play concerns a threatened violation of Virginia's 'honour', there is little talk of honour in the abstract. Instead, the emphasis remains on natural filial and paternal affection and—clearly a subsidiary value—on the natural love of a young man and woman for one another. *Virginius* maintains a consistent tone of high seriousness. Pathos arises first from the very fact that Virginius is a widower, his daughter Virginia half an orphan, and Knowles makes much of the fact that this is a motherless family. The death of the mother years before has tightened the bond between father and daughter, but, as the tragic situation

[17] See Donohue, *Dramatic Character*, Pt. I and, for analyses of *Evadne*, *Bertram*, and *Fazio*, pp. 35–42, 88–91 and 169–172.

evolves and Virginia's chastity is threatened by an unprincipled tyrant, it appears impossible to prove that Virginia is really the deceased mother's child. Consequently, the perjured testimony of a suborned female slave that she sold Virginia as a baby to Virginius' childless wife cannot be controverted except through Virginius' own ineffectual denials. The theme of the play, then, concerns the helplessness of family ties and natural human affection in the face of lawlessness, construed in what is apparently its most menacing form: sexual lust.

In this respect an interesting analogy is operating in the dramatic structure. The political aspect of the plot concerns the tyranny of the Decemvir Appius and the mounting wrath and ultimate revolt of the citizenry against him. But in the context of the 'inner' action of the play, Appius' tyranny may be read as a sign for the lust instantaneously aroused in him when he first sees Virginius' angelically beautiful daughter. He determines to have her, and when his henchman Claudius is unsuccessful at bribing Virginia's nurse, Claudius conceives of the ruse involving his slave's perjured testimony. Virginius being absent in the wars, we now see Claudius dragging the extremely distraught Virginia through the streets of Rome. Virginius is informed and instantly returns, and in Act IV a bitter confrontation takes place between Virginius and Appius. Knowles protracts the climax, so that we slowly but surely see Virginius' defences—all of them reasonable, all sanctioned time out of mind by English life—crumble. No honest plea can touch the ear of this corrupt administration, let alone an appeal as righteous as this of Virginius':

> Look not on Claudius—look on your Decemvir!
> He is the master claims Virginia!
> The tongues that told him she was not my child
> Are these—the costly charms he cannot purchase,
> Except by making her the slave of Claudius,
> His client, his purveyor, that caters for
> His pleasures—markets for him—picks, and scents,
> And tastes, that he may banquet—serves him up
> His sensual feast, and is not now asham'd,
> In the open, common street, before your eyes—

139

> Frighting your daughters and your matrons' cheeks
> With blushes they ne'er thought to meet—to help him
> To the honour of a Roman maid! my child!

When nothing else avails, Virginius lights on a desperate remedy. As the stage directions explain, '*at length his eye falls on a butcher's stall, with a knife upon it*'. Momentarily concealing the weapon in his tunic and moving close to Virginia, he cries out, 'There is one only way to save thine honour— / 'Tis this!' and stabs his daughter to death.[18]

In other hands the whole of Act V might have proved an anticlimax, and even Knowles, whose instincts are sound, is forced to extreme measures. Appius, condemned to prison, is visited by a pathetic Virginius entirely bereft of his reason, so stricken is he by the murder of his own daughter. The moment, verging on the thin edge of the ludicrous, was perhaps compelling in the convention-prone atmosphere of a proscenium theatre:

> *Virginius.*　　　　　　I am wild, distracted, mad!
> I am all a flame—a flame! I tell thee once
> For all, I want my child, and I will have her;
> So give her to me.
> *Appius.*　　　　　　Cag'd with a madman! Hoa!
> Without there![19]

Virginius' distraction is the only adequate counterbalance to the desperate deed he has committed. Moreover, it invites us to excuse Virginius' murder of Appius, which now ensues offstage. Knowles's own ingenuous explanation makes the point clear:

After having excited such an interest for Virginius, it would have been indecent to represent him in the attitude of taking the law into his own hands. I therefore adopted the idea of his destroying Appius in a fit of temporary insanity, which gives the catastrophe the air of a visitation of Providence.[20]

[18] *Virginius: A Tragedy*, 2nd edn. (1820), IV.ii, p. 67.
[19] V.iii, p. 81.　　　　　　　　　　　　　　　[20] Preface.

Only when presented with his daughter's ashes does Virginius, whom we see at the end of the play standing over the mute form of Appius, return to his senses and realize that Virginia is indeed dead. The sign of his restoration to normality is, as heavy precedent demands, his newly regained ability to weep.

In a passage of fulsome praise for Knowles, Hazlitt described the playwright as a sort of primitive, ignorant of the rules of art, producing a perfect work by obeying 'the impulses of natural feeling'. That Knowles was evidently able to stir the same impulses in his audience explains in a general way the success of his tragedy. More specifically, its peculiar force-fulness may be owing to its clarity as a parable of the values of English domestic life. Hazlitt gets the orientation of the play just right in describing the character of its author. 'Mr. Knowles is the first tragic writer of the age,' he said, but 'in other respects he is a common man; and divides his time and his affections between his plots and his fishing-tackle'. . . .[21]

Plays like *Virginius*, set in classical or medieval Rome or elsewhere in Italy and dealing importantly with politics and government, are as a group the clearest aspirants in the period to dramatic legitimacy, a desideratum that so preoccupied the age that even a realistic morality play like Buckstone's *Victorine* (Adelphi, 17 October 1831) was admired as 'a species of the regular drama'.[22] The relationship of these plays to political issues current in contemporary England is less clear but of possibly great significance. Dramas on classical subjects had of course been a standard part of the English repertory since Tudor times, and authors as diverse as Shakespeare, Jonson, Lee, Addison and Whitehead had all expended energies on them. So too, in the early nineteenth century, did other authors in addition to Knowles and Byron: John Howard Payne, Mary Russell Mitford, Thomas Talford, and some lesser writers such as Thomas Henry Lister. Two of the more prominent tragedies in this idiom, Payne's *Brutus; or, The Fall of Tarquin* (Drury Lane, 3 December 1818) and Mitford's *Rienzi* (Drury Lane, 9 October 1828) have in common a plot that

[21] *The Spirit of the Age*, in Hazlitt, XI, 184.
[22] *Report*, Q. 2950.

centres on a right-minded citizen who takes over and purges a corrupt government but then is faced with an agonizing and possibly compromising decision about a loved one's life. No hint of direct political allusion surfaces here, or elsewhere. The Lord Chamberlain's licencers John Larpent and, later, the younger George Colman maintained an effective censorship. Yet the very repetitiveness of plays about conspiracy, misplaced loyalties and the conflicting claims of public and private duty suggests that they stand in some parabolic relationship to important issues of the time. In this pre-Reform period, such treatments (admittedly oblique) of the problematic connection between the rule of law and domestic life may well have held an interest whose significance might be recaptured by careful study.

For these and other reasons, the plays of the early nineteenth century repay attention, despite the discomfort they seem to produce in unengaged readers of dramatic literature. Granted, they may incite unintended pain or laughter, just as some did for their original audiences. Still, it remains arguable that the proper study of the theatre encompasses values that are social, moral, political and intellectual, as well as literary and aesthetic. These values, as reflected in the texts of individual plays of the early nineteenth century, can best be observed if the theatre itself is acknowledged to exist in a lengthy and wide historical continuum. The nineteenth century was an age of unparalleled development and expansion. We are beginning to understand that the growth of the theatre was one of the most significant aspects of this change, and beginning to surmise that the drama produced in this theatre was instrumental to it. We do not know precisely how, but the materials for determining this have survived and lie ready for scrutiny. Served by a more cogent historiography of the drama, historians may eventually gather and interpret sufficient evidence to justify the intuition of present students that the age of Edmund Kean was not only a complex age, but one of real, if controversial, dramatic vitality.

CHAPTER EIGHT

Critics and Audiences

Among the theatre audiences of early nineteenth-century London were persons whose habit of playgoing had nourished a positive critical attitude towards the drama of the age and of ages past. Undoubtedly those viewers were by nature unreluctant to express opinions, but a certain few had the opportunity to do so in the pages of the public press. From beginnings early in the previous century, the profession of theatre critic had grown to a position of importance and influence in the age of Kean. Although normally the audience itself determined, on the spot, the success of every performance, the regular appearance of critical reviews in the daily, weekly and monthly press had become a significant phenomenon.

This widespread attention in print to performed drama mirrored a great popular interest in the subject. Readers of newspapers as well established as *The Times*, *Morning Chronicle* and *Public Advertiser*, and of periodicals as diverse as the *Gentleman's Magazine*, *Monthly Mirror* and *Examiner* evidently wanted to know what was going on in the contemporary theatre. An additional index of literate interest in theatrical production, even more noteworthy in view of the alleged decline of the literary drama itself, was the appearance in increasing numbers of periodicals devoted exclusively to theatrical concerns. Two of the most important early serials were Thomas Dutton's *Dramatic Censor; or, Weekly Theatrical Report* (1800–01) and Thomas Holcroft's *Theatrical Recorder* (1805). These and other theatrical periodicals of the time were concerned with reportage of daily activity, but consistently this information was combined with biographical, historical and other materials that reflected an aspiration towards serious criticism and a sense of its larger implications. *The Dramatic Censor; or, Critical and Biographical Illustration of the British Stage*, which appeared monthly during 1811, asserted on its title page the editor's purpose 'to sustain the morality and dignity of the drama'.[1] Between 1800 and 1830 some one hundred and sixty different periodicals devoted exclusively to the theatre came into existence throughout Great Britain—over five times as many as had been published since Richard Steele established the species with *The Theatre* in 1720. Aside from the sheer number, what is impressive is the enthusiasm they generate for their subject and the tenacity that characterizes their playgoing critics, who in at least some cases were fully the equal of their brethren on the staffs of daily newspapers. Although some wrote weekly or only occasionally, others were contributing to a burgeoning daily theatrical press. By 1825 some nineteen daily theatrical periodicals had appeared, and not only in London, but in Dublin, Liverpool and Edinburgh.[2]

With little time for second thoughts, most of their reviewers were pragmatists who met deadlines by serving up the standard fare familiar to readers since the century before. If the piece was new, the format consisted of a plot summary, often detailed, followed by judicial strictures or praise in which action, language and 'sentiments' were by turns anatomized; finally, the performances of actor and actress were scrutinized. A new mounting of an old play would be judged for its novelty, but here as always the emphasis tended to remain on the performances of individual players. Inevitably, the repertory system afforded opportunity for close critical comparison of one performance of an established role with another, or of a

---

[1] See Carl J. Stratman, C.S.V., *Britain's Theatrical Periodicals 1720–1967* (New York, 1972), p. 8.
[2] Stratman, *Britain's Theatrical Periodicals*, pp. 9–16.

given role with other performances by the same actor or actress. Such criticism was by necessity descriptive, yet unmistakably judicial, and ever sensitive to the immediate effect of the player on an audience. A paragraph on the success of Cooper as Octavian in *The Mountaineers* illustrates the typical vocabulary and representative assumptions and values of contemporary reviewers: 'The wanderings of a naturally powerful intellect, under the influence of a vivid imagination, kindled by the burning heat of a devouring passion, were finely drawn in the abrupt transitions which marked each sudden change of thought: but the best effort was the expression of the frenzied ecstasy of sudden joy, contending with the strong and stifling emotions of long cherished grief, on the sudden interview with *Floranthe*. It was well imagined, and striking in its execution, and drew down repeated peals of applause.'[3]

The assessment is essentially a balanced one, although high in its praise. In practice, of course, such criticism could also be extremely subjective and unpredictable. Then as now, a large proportion of theatrical journalism was at the least undistinguished, and some was heavily biased (gratuitously, or for a price), supercilious, condescending, reactionary or just grossly ignorant. The sheer difficulty of the enterprise was, and remains, formidable. 'There is perhaps no task,' said the *Theatrical Observer* in 1821, 'in which the vanity or interest of man engages, that is so little understood, more generally assumed, or that requires higher and more expansive qualifications for its just discharge than does the *task* of *criticism*.'[4]

Some few writers were equal to the challenge. And, in an age of great acting, it seems natural that the best efforts of theatrical critics emerged in close description of actors and actresses. Workaday critics like Thomas Barnes, who wrote for Leigh Hunt's *Examiner*, could intermittently rise to the occasion, as when Barnes was asked to report on Kean as Macbeth.[5] For consistent perceptiveness, however, there were

[3] Unsigned review in *The Drama; or, Theatrical Pocket Magazine*, 1 (1821), p. 196. [4] *Theatrical Observer*, 2 (3 November 1821), p. 2.
[5] See the *Examiner*, 15 November 1814.

three critics unmatched in the period: William Hazlitt, Leigh Hunt and Charles Lamb. Each had a style, a character, uniquely his own.

While still a young man Hunt asserted a claim to notice in his *Critical Essays on the Performers of the London Theatres* (1807). His enthusiasms and dislikes are everywhere evident but are accompanied by carefully measured judgements and astute insights. Hunt is at his best in summarizing the overall impression of an actor in performance, as in his description of John Kemble:

For the expression of the loftier emotions no actor is gifted by nature with greater external means. His figure though not elegant is manly and dignified, his features are strongly marked with what is called the Roman character, and his head altogether is the heroic head of the antiquary and the artist. This tragic form assumes excellently well the gait of royalty, the vigorous majesty of the warrior, and the profound gravity of the sage; but it's seriousness is unbending; his countenance seems to despise the gaiety it labours to assume, and it's comic expression is comic because it is singularly wretched.[6]

It is illuminating to place this passage alongside Hazlitt's description of the same actor, on the occasion of Kemble's retirement in 1817:

If he had not the unexpected bursts of nature and genius, he had all the regularity of art; if he did not display the tumult and conflict of opposite passions in the soul, he gave the deepest and most permanent interest to the uninterrupted progress of individual feeling; and in embodying a high idea of certain characters, which belong rather to sentiment than passion, to energy of will, than to loftiness or to originality of imagination, he was the most excellent actor of his time.[7]

Although it may seem unfair to compare Hunt in his youth with Hazlitt in his prime, the greater comprehensiveness of Hazlitt's sense of human nature implicit in dramatic character

[6] Hunt, *Critical Essays*, pp. 5–6.
[7] Hazlitt, V, 379.

is a measure of his absolute pre-eminence over Hunt. Hazlitt was unassailably the foremost critic of his time.

Yet both Hunt and Hazlitt were accomplished in the kind of minute description that all but recreates the art itself. 'The genius of folly,' Hazlitt said of Liston's comic acting, 'spreads its shining gloss over his face, tickles his nose, laughs in his eyes, makes his teeth chatter in his head, or draws up every muscle into a look of indescribable dulness, or freezes his whole person into a lump of ice (as in Lubin Log) or relaxes it into the very thaw and dissolution of all common sense (as in his Lord Grizzle).'[8] Only Charles Lamb could excel at this task, as he does in a brilliant description of Munden as Old Dozey in Dibdin's farce *Past Ten O'Clock*:

Old Dozey is a plant from Greenwich. The bronzed face—and neck to match,—the long curtain of a coat—the straggling white hair,—the propensity,—the determined attachment, to grog,—are all from Greenwich. Munden, as Dozey, seems never to have been out of action, sun, and drink!—He looks (alas! he *looked*) fire proof. His face and throat were dried like a raisin—and his legs walked under the rum and water with all the indecision which that inestimable beverage usually inspires. It is truly tacking, not walking. He *steers* at a table, and the tide of grog now and then bears him off the point. On this night he seemed to us to be doomed to fall in action. . . .[9]

Whereas Hunt specialized in doing justice to the immediate theatrical experience, Lamb's genius was one of reminiscence. Hazlitt's forte, in contrast, made him an anomaly among reviewers, a philosophical critic. While Leigh Hunt was occupying his early days with journalism and a book on the London performers, Hazlitt's first publication of any length was *An Essay on the Principles of Human Action* (1805), in which he argued for the 'natural disinterestedness of the human mind'. It is no distortion to view his entire output as a reviewer in the light of his early philosophical predilections. His sense of tragic character, for example, may be understood to a considerable extent in terms of the character's egotistical

[8] Hazlitt, XVIII, 403.
[9] *London Magazine*, July 1824, in Lamb, I, 379.

deviation from a disinterested view of the world. What makes Hazlitt most interesting as a theatrical critic is his deep feeling for human nature and the root causes of human conduct. The same quality makes him less than a reliable guide to day-by-day theatrical production. His interests transcend the journalistic, and he sometimes dismisses work of considerable skill and effort in a grudging phrase or two in order to get on with an extensive description of an archetypal character, played by an actor who doesn't suit with the ideal.

Occasionally, however, such comparisons did justice both to character and performer. The fortuitous conjunction of Edmund Kean with one of Shakespeare's, or perhaps Massinger's, heroes conspired to bring 'out the best in this moody, fiercely independent writer. 'The character of Shylock,' Hazlitt said in writing of Kean's London debut in the role in 1814, 'is that of a man brooding over one idea, that of its wrongs, and bent on one unalterable purpose, that of revenge.' In measuring Kean against that standard, he concluded that the actor was not ideally cast, but there were compensations that more than made up for the deficiency. The enthusiasm with which Hazlitt praised Kean's declamation, rapidity of transition, and ability to delight and surprise an audience with 'a succession of striking pictures'[10] suggests how fully Hazlitt had found an interpreter of Shakespeare after his own heart.

Kean's most successful Shakespearean role was that of Richard the Third (presented, as unvarying tradition dictated, in Cibber's streamlined version). Hazlitt seized the opportunity presented in Kean's Macbeth, first acted in the autumn of 1814, to give his readers a comprehensive philosophical assessment of the distinctions between the characters of Macbeth and Richard. Unlike Macbeth, he explained, Richard is not an imaginative character, but one who acts from sheer force of will, or passion. No conflict of feelings blunts his single-mindedness of purpose. Consequently, Kean's manner of playing Richard was for Hazlitt one of the supreme accomplishments attained in the theatre of his day, and the quintessence of it appeared in the death scene:

148 [10] Hazlitt, V, 179.

He fought like one drunk with wounds: and the attitude in which he stands with his hands stretched out, after his sword is taken from him, had a preternatural and terrific grandeur, as if his will could not be disarmed, and the very phantoms of his despair had a withering power.[11]

The other side of Kean's brilliant success here, however, was the actor's failure—as Hazlitt saw it—in Macbeth. The failure was almost inevitable, considering Hazlitt's view of Macbeth himself as the archetypal Romantic hero, whose actions stem from the powerful stimulus of his own imaginative transformation of the world about him into the agency of his fortunate rise. Perhaps no actor could have represented psychological subtlety and profound imaginativeness of this kind on the cavernous reaches of the Drury Lane stage. Kean, at any rate, did not, Hazlitt found, despite the intellectual éclat that in general distinguished his roles. Although he may not have done full justice to Kean, it is Hazlitt's sense of failure that makes his criticism extraordinarily significant. That he could write such pieces under the pressure of impending deadlines suggests the reach of his own intellect and the depth of his conviction that dramatic performance has a central place in the life of the mind.

Convictions of that sort make Hazlitt worth reading but at the same time highly untypical of those people who, night by night, made their way to Drury Lane, Covent Garden, and other places of theatrical entertainment in or around London. As fully as the theatre may feed intellectual pursuits, it is just as likely to scorn them in favour of what must be any theatre's first and foremost concern, its paying audience.

Too little is known about the audiences of early nineteenth-century London theatres. Although convenient generalizations abound, they in some cases obscure our view of the complex and inconsistent realities of theatrical attendance in the age. For example, it is well known that the overall social composition of the audience changed markedly in the course of the twenty-five years beginning about 1790. All the evidence points towards this conclusion, but it is more an aid to

[11] Hazlitt, V, 182.

description than a means for analysis. Until thorough research has pieced together a coherent picture of the identities and behaviour of audiences in this period and related it significantly to contemporary social history and specific demographic data, our understanding will remain fragmentary. All the same, it is possible to describe to some extent the nature of the theatregoing public in this time, bearing in mind that the relationship between player and playgoer affects the significance of the evidence.

In the time of Kean, as in that of Garrick and Betterton before him, the English theatre was a tripartite physical entity composed of pit, box and gallery. So deeply entrenched was this division of the seating area that the deliberate omission of boxes from the new Sans Pareil (later the Adelphi), which opened late in 1806, had to be speedily remedied. Despite a certain mobility reflected in the seating choices made by some members of this audience, the fact remains that boxes, pits and galleries contained a socially stratified assembly. In selecting one or another of these three possibilities, patrons had in effect identified themselves, at least for the evening, as being of a certain class of spectator.

What happened as the nineteenth century progressed was that these traditional divisions began to reflect a deepening conflict between the more traditional aristocratic and comfortably middle-class elements of Garrick's and Sheridan's audience and the less literate, more unruly classes of a swelling urban population. The strange conjunctions of mainpiece and afterpiece often found in patent theatre bills in the first decades of the new century attest to management's feverish attempt to cater to the heterogeneous tastes of an audience engaged in sometimes bitter dispute. The advancement of the dinner hour for gentlemen of fashion to half-price time by the 1830s[12] suggests the degree to which upper-class elements had deserted the theatre, driven out partly by the unpalatable fare presented in addition to or in lieu of the old classics, and partly by the increasing, and increasingly noticeable, presence of persons they considered disreputable. Among these were prostitutes

[12] *Report*, Q. 1058.

and their prey, as John Adolphus explained, who formerly had
been present but kept discreetly separate:

The dress-boxes in the old theatre were exclusively occupied by those
who could sustain the appearance required at an evening party of the
first character. The front-boxes, and the tier above the dress-boxes,
called the green-boxes, were filled, for the most part, with families
and individuals of respectable station in life; and, if persons of
character not quite so unequivocal found places in them, they were
bound to the utmost propriety of demeanour. The upper boxes, or
slips, were left to the females who frequent play-houses as a mart for
their charms, and the tavern-haunting youths who went with the
intention of becoming their customers.

The great advantage of this old arrangement, Adolphus said,
was that no parent would ever be forced to lead his family out
of the theatre 'through a lane of immodest females and
licentious coxcombs', for the stairs, lobbies and other avenues
of egress were maintained in strictest propriety.[13] The public
boxes themselves, according to another writer whose comment
dates from 1822, had by this time been infiltrated by
disreputable elements, with the result that the opera house
was the sole place where one could see a theatre 'filled with
elegant and beautiful women'.[14]

Under the circumstances, the increased desirability of
private boxes and the patent managements' assiduous efforts
to provide more of them—as in the 1794 Drury Lane, where
portions of former gallery space were taken over for this
purpose—were quite understandable. Testifying at the 1832
Parliamentary inquiry, Peter Laporte, manager and proprietor
of Covent Garden, observed that private boxes were 'clearly
an advantage for the sake of the higher classes of society', who
often would simply not attend the theatre unless they had
access to one, with its completely separate entrance.[15] Such
boxes could occasionally be had, seasonally or nightly, from
the box-office, but were coveted enough to be occasionally

[13] John Adolphus, *Memoirs of John Bannister, Comedian* (1839), I, 258–259.
[14] Unidentified clipping in Hawkins, III, f. 22.
[15] *Report*, Q. 2239.

sold at auction.[16] A sense of the questionable activity that could sometimes go on in these boxes, shielded as they were from public view, is perhaps discernable in the comment of an anonymous critic who one night forsook his customary position in the pit to see Kean's Sir Giles Overreach from a box. Finding the experience decidedly unpleasant, he observed that no part of the theatre 'is so thoroughly wrapped up in itself and fortified against any impression from what is passing on the stage'. The rule in the boxes, he concluded, is that of 'fashionable indifference'.[17]

Typically, then, the posture of the patent managers was the duplicitous one of having to condescend to the demands of the gallery while desperately cultivating the reluctant attendance of an often too well-mannered higher-class audience. It had in fact become more and more clear that the gallery was the section most essential for any theatre manager to please. Some persons, like John Adolphus, considered the front row in the two-shilling gallery of the older theatre the most preferable for sheer enjoyment of the play.[18] In Lamb's delightful essay 'Old China', Elia's cousin Bridget remembers with relish those days when poverty enforced only infrequent attendance and the purchase of a one-shilling gallery seat. 'You used to say,' she recalls, 'that the gallery was the best place of all for enjoying a play socially, . . . that the company we met there, not being in general readers of plays, were obliged to attend the more, and did attend, to what was going on, on the stage—because a word lost would have been a chasm, which it was impossible for them to fill up.'[19] From the plays cited it seems likely that Lamb has in mind the little theatre in the Haymarket in the 1790s. Forty years later the importance of the gallery audience there continued to be felt. Asked during the 1832 Parliamentary inquiry whether the Haymarket might consider doing away with the galleries and making private boxes there to accommodate the fashionable world, D. E. Morris, the

[16] Covent Garden playbill, 14 December 1818; advertisement of auction (Folger Shakespeare Library).   [17] Hawkins, II, f. 71.

[18] Adolphus, *Memoirs of Bannister*, I, 259.

[19] *London Magazine* (March 1823), in Lamb, II, 250.

proprietor, replied that such an experiment would entail great risk and that even greater losses would probably be the result.[20] Clearly the gallery was the backbone of the theatre, to be ignored or slighted only at peril.

Unlettered and disorderly as they often were, gallerygoers took with them to the theatre an inimitable enthusiasm that, to a lesser extent, characterized the pit audience as well. On the occasion of Elliston's Haymarket benefit in 1804 Elliston had hired the larger, more commodious King's Opera. His optimism was justified, for, by as early as five o'clock, the crowd had forced the doors off their hinges and had 'poured into the theatre at every aperture, like water into a wreck, and in a few minutes there was an overflow in pit and boxes, which found its level at no less an elevation than the ceiling'.[21] In 1830, on the occasion of Kean's farewell prior to an American tour, the same theatre was besieged by a huge number of persons clambering for entrance, and the situation appeared conducive to the survival of only the fittest. 'As the hour for opening the doors more nearly approached,' recalled a spectator, 'the heat of the atmosphere, the dense pressure of the crowd, the nauseous and filthily impregnated air, which all were breathing, and the feverish cries for relief' made the scene comparable to conditions 'in the black hole at Calcutta'.[22] Elia was certainly not exaggerating the relief and satisfaction felt by 'poor gallery scramblers' who could finally utter a 'delicious *Thank God, we are safe*, which always followed when the topmost stair, conquered, let in the first light of the whole cheerful theatre down beneath us'. . . .[23]

Once ensconced, the gallery audience was ready for a full evening's entertainment and prepared to be well entertained or to know the reason why not. Traditionally the gallery was the most vociferous segment of the theatre audience, never too inhibited to call out for what pleased them most. Playing *Macbeth* at Bristol in 1803, John Kemble attempted to omit the

[20] *Report*, Q. 2503.
[21] Raymond, *Memoirs of Elliston*, I, 255.
[22] Unidentified clipping dated [July 1830] in Hawkins, III, f. 328.
[23] Lamb, II, 252.

long-traditional dance of witches with their brooms but was required to restore it when the gallery put up such a disturbance that the play could not otherwise proceed, and the same thing happened when he moved on to Bath and its supposedly more polite audience.[24] Sometimes individual members of the assembly in the 'heavens' could create a considerable annoyance, as did two men forced to apologize in the playbill for having thrown 'Apples, Orange Peel, &c.' at the audience in the pit during a performance in 1813.[25] Graceless behaviour was not, of course, the prerogative of any one segment of the audience. Lamb complained to readers of the *London Magazine* of the 'dapper warehouseman' and others sitting at their ease in the pit and jeering at the distress of a homely woman who had to stand for lack of a place. No claim for gallantry in the theatre could be made, Lamb added, until gentlemen no longer felt free to hiss an offending actress off the stage.[26]

From very early times, however, hissing a player and damning a play had remained the traditional right of the British playgoer, the unquestioned arbiter of theatrical taste. Thomas Holcroft's opinion was that managers themselves brought on their audience's extreme acrimoniousness by advertising condemned plays as having been received 'with loud and universal applause'.[27] In any case, the public were the judge, first and last, and ever less reluctant to express their feelings. Playing Pizarro to Kemble's Rolla at Covent Garden in 1803, George Frederick Cooke attempted to apologize for what was in fact his habitual drunkenness by citing 'my old complaint, my old complaint', but the only result was irresistible laughter throughout the house, 'and amidst roars, shouts and hisses he retired'.[28] Most reactions of this kind were spontaneous, but some were the planned consequences of rivalry between players or enmity between managers or

[24] Genest, VII, 596–597.
[25] Playbill, 26 Feb. 1813, Theatre Royal, Exeter, in Hawkins, I, opp. f. 138.
[26] *London Magazine* (November 1822), in Lamb, II, 79–80.
[27] *Theatrical Recorder*, I (1805), p. 126.
[28] Genest, VII, 612.

dramatists. Noisy fellows from Drury Lane were quite capable of disrupting the performance of a new play or the debut of a new player at Covent Garden, either out of sheer spite or, some might allege, for monetary gain. The younger George Colman observed in 1818 that, owing to Kean's great success in the role and his consolidation of a partisan audience, no debutant could appear in Richard the Third without an antagonistic party arriving to 'explode' him on his first entrance.[29] In less special circumstances, Colman explained, hypercritical elements in an audience unjustifiably damn plays that have no pretension to anything except honest, exuberant laughter.[30] It sometimes appeared that the so-called 'monster of the pit' was a denizen of a no-man's-land unaccountably hostile to friend and foe alike.

In extreme instances, simple bad manners could give way to more riotous behaviour, especially dangerous in the crowded conditions of indoor public assembly. Sometimes lives were at stake, sometimes principles, as in the case of the 'O. P. Riots', conducted on a scale previously unmatched by a vengefully determined nucleus of outraged playgoers. Colman thought it inevitable that a body of persons invested, however unofficially, with such powers of decisive judgement might well not always exercise them with restraint or good sense.[31] It sometimes appeared that almost anything, even the apparently innocuous, could cause disorder to erupt. In 1805, Dowton's Haymarket benefit piece *The Tailors* drew a large contingent of tailors who considered this burlesque an offence to their craft. Guards and constables twice had to put down the disturbance, fomented by journeymen in the gallery above and masters in the pit below, and some seventy persons were taken into custody.[32] Earlier that same year the management of the King's Opera attempted to curtail the Saturday evening performance of a post-operatic ballet in compliance with an injunction from certain reforming bishops not to violate the Sabbath. The

[29] Colman, II, 257.
[30] Colman, II, 57.
[31] Colman, II, 252.
[32] *Theatrical Recorder*, 2 (1805), p. 207.

dropping of the curtain at half-past eleven occasioned an immediate call for the dance to continue, and when members of the orchestra ignored it and closed their books, one book was seized and flung on the stage. It was the signal for action:

A number of persons crowded on the stage. The book was flung back into the pit, and the manager was called for. Mr. Kelly came forward to explain the conduct of the house, and respectfully to state that they could only bow with submission to the injunctions that had been given them. But he was not heard. The audience called for the bishops who had given the orders; and Mr. Kelly was struck a violent blow. He defended himself, and was with difficulty rescued by some gentlemen who interfered in his favor. The tumult now increased to an outrageous attack on the chandeliers, benches, musical instruments, and every thing else within reach, and the theatre was threatened with utter demolition. Considerable damage was done, and it was with difficulty that the affray was quelled.[33]

Over the course of the first quarter of the nineteenth century the limits of inappropriate behaviour of audiences were, it would seem, extended again and again. Yet it is all too easy to exaggerate the degree of excessiveness. The highly decorous silence maintained by twentieth-century audiences, cloaked in the anonymity of darkened auditoriums, was simply not the norm in the eighteenth or nineteenth century. An audience that can see the auditorium as well as the stage during a performance is one very much aware of itself and more easily inclined towards generally vocal behaviour. Judged by this norm, the audiences of Kean's day were an orderly crowd, by and large, ready to forgive and forget the instant their wishes had been heard and obeyed. In some cases fanatically loyal, they were habitual playgoers, many of them; it was, after all, for such frequenters of pit, box and gallery that the repertory system had evolved, with its combination of the familiar and the novel arranged nightly for continued satisfaction.

These generalities hold, it seems, for the theatregoing populace of London as a whole, although examples of typical or aberrant behaviour are most easily found for the major

[33] *Morning Chronicle*, quoted in the *Theatrical Recorder*, 2 (1805), pp. 67–68.

theatres—Drury Lane, Covent Garden, the little Haymarket and the King's Opera. Yet the fact is that, however much our impression remains of an essentially homogeneous audience, it is far from being either the undifferentiated monolith of some accounts or the totally divided one of others. Partial information must serve, for the present, in delineating differences between one section of London and another and between theatre and theatre.

For it is true that, in some cases, even theatre managers themselves were unsure of the identities of their audiences, or at least were reluctant to describe them. During the 1832 Parliamentary inquiry the following exchange took place, with D. E. Morris, proprietor of the Haymarket, in the witness chair:

Are not the audiences at your theatre composed of a different set of persons, and people who reside at a different part of the town, from the audiences that attend the Coburg theatre?—I cannot exactly answer that question; our theatre is well situated; but there are persons of good condition visiting those minor theatres.

Is the audience as respectable at the Coburg theatre as it is at yours?—Sometimes it may be, and at other times perhaps not.[34]

Morris might well be accused of evasiveness, not wishing to alienate anyone with the price of admission to his theatre, but it remains true that any audience is a mixed group, differing from night to night. J. P. Collier thought that transpontine audiences were very likely 'more ignorant and worse informed' than others closer in,[35] but G. B. Davidge, proprietor of the Coburg in 1832, maintained that Monday night working-class audiences at his theatre were succeeded in the middle of the week by 'the better classes, the play-going public generally'. Even the nobility, including the Lord Chamberlain himself, attend, Davidge added, taking both public and private boxes.[36] Earlier in his testimony Davidge described his patrons as coming from the west end and the City, observing that they included 'most of the royal family'.[37]

[34] *Report*, Qq. 2442–43.   [35] *Report*, Q. 427.
[36] *Report*, Qq. 1270–77.   [37] *Report*, Qq. 1204–5.

On the other hand, T. P. Cooke, who had acted at the Coburg, pointed out that its audience, like others in outlying districts, was essentially a local one. It was possible that gallerygoers at the Coburg might also frequent the major theatres, he allowed, but the Coburg audience as a whole was 'almost restricted to that theatre' and essentially different from that of the Surrey, despite its short distance away.[38] Testifying on the subject of Surrey audiences, David Osbaldiston, its proprietor and manager, explained that the theatre attracted persons from all parts but that a preponderance came from the vicinity.[39] Despite sometimes exaggerated claims, there seems little doubt that theatres across the Thames could not consistently draw significant portions of the general London audience. On occasion, a fashionable audience might be irresistibly attracted to some special entertainment. Thomas Dibdin recalled that his dramatization of Walter Scott's novel under the title *The Heart of Midlothian; or, The Lily of St. Leonards* for the Surrey in 1813 brought a flow of congratulatory letters, and 'carriages of the first nobility graced the road in nightly lines, sometimes double'. . . .[40] Evidently, the general rule was one of local support, as T. J. Serle confirmed, citing in particular the Pavilion in the East End and the Coburg, which he said drew 'decidedly from its own neighborhood'. In contrast, however, Astley's special mode of equestrian entertainment drew audiences from every part of town.[41]

Whatever their exact make-up, audiences were attending the minor theatres in significant numbers, and complaints from major theatre managers became more audible as the theatres generally entered on a period of financial difficulty in the third decade of the century. Charles Kemble told the 1832 Parliamentary committee that the major theatres were not at all full, owing, he felt, to the 'stronger excitement, and coarser species of entertainment at a much cheaper rate' available at the minor houses.[42] T. P. Cooke held another point of view,

[38] *Report*, Qq. 2606–7.
[39] *Report*, Qq. 1596–97.
[40] Dibdin, *Reminiscences*, II, 157.
[41] *Report*, Qq. 2131–33.   [42] *Report*, Q. 627.

observing that at least on benefit nights the audience of the City Theatre in Finsbury was quite kind and well disposed—'a gallery kind of audience'.[43] The singer John Braham considered that the gallery audience at major theatres had latterly improved, allowing the introduction of Italian music in addition to ballads, which he believed always had 'a beauty and an appeal' to all except those 'who pretend to be fashionable, and to despise the voice of nature'.[44]

The nucleus of the theatrical audience was, as ever, an appreciative group to whom the basic appeal of the theatrical experience itself was seldom made in vain. If melodramas and spectacles have become the popular favourites of the generality of theatregoers, said the *Theatrical Observer* in 1821, this 'degeneracy of taste' can be blamed directly on the managers themselves for having cultivated it.[45] A biased and not very intelligent analysis, a comment of this sort reflects once again the perplexing emergence of a newer audience on whom the traditional repertory of dramatic tragedy and comedy was allegedly a waste. Such a judgement was easy to make, no doubt, once one had seen at close range some of the wretched, shallow stuff that had to a degree supplanted Jonson, Addison and Sheridan. But the circumstances did not admit of easy judgements. Anyone wishing to dismiss the performances at minor theatres as beneath serious consideration would first have to deal with the possibilities implied in the testimony of Edmund L. Swifte, keeper of the Crown Jewels, at the 1832 Inquiry:

I have observed lately that when I have gone to the minor theatres, where certainly the audience is composed of what I should call (if I may say so without offence) the lower part of the middle classes, I have observed that every exhibition of the regular drama, or any exhibition at all approaching to the performance of the regular drama, has been more felt and more liked by the audience than any mere spectacle or buffoonery has been, and from thence I infer that there is among us a great regard for the national drama. . . .[46]

[43] *Report*, Q. 2628.   [44] *Report*, Q. 1565.
[45] *Theatrical Observer*, 1 (30 October 1821), p. 125.   [46] *Report*, Q. 2942.

One recalls that the miserable level of some of the earlier pieces at the minor theatres was caused as much by the legal prohibition of legitimate drama as by any other factor. The phenomenal growth of minor theatres in the early nineteenth century and the extensive adjustments this occasioned in the conduct of the majors are a reminder that the foremost requirement for any theatre management is to discover and draw an audience, and then to hold it, by whatever means. One cannot educate empty seats. Yet one can appeal to basic needs and desires—as melodrama arguably does—without necessarily forgoing either tradition or sanity. Thomas Dibdin explained how the process worked, recalling the conversion of Home's *Douglas* to Surrey melodrama. This tragedy, he said,

without omitting a single line of the author, made a very splendid melo-drama, with the additions of Lord Randolph's magnificent banquet, a martial Scotch dance, and a glee, formed from Home's words,—'Free is his heart who for his country fights, &c. &c.' exquisitely set by Sanderson, and delightfully sung, together with an expensive processional representation of the landing of the Danes: besides all this, as a Surrey Theatre gallery audience always expects some *ultra* incident, I had a representative of Lady Randolph in the person of a very clever boy, by whose good acting and fearless agility, the northern dame, at the conclusion of the tragedy, was seen to throw herself from a distant precipice into a boiling ocean, in a style which literally brought down thunders of applause.[47]

Accommodation might be not only the price of survival but the means of reviving a languishing theatre. If this was in fact what was taking place, the impetus had come not so much from the professionals on the far side of the proscenium arch as from the *amateurs* who gathered before it. Fickle, tyrannical and impossibly noisy as they often were, the audiences of the early nineteenth century nevertheless shared a vitality that gave character to all they did and beyond which, like it or not, there would never be any appeal.

[47] Dibdin, *Reminiscences*, II, 170.

CHAPTER NINE

Plays, Poems and Readers

By the late seventeenth century the habit of reading plays, encouraged by the interdiction of theatrical performance during the Commonwealth period, had become well enough established for John Dryden to be able to explain, 'As 'tis my Interest to please my Audience, so 'tis my Ambition to be read'. . . .[1] In the half-century that followed, the habit persisted and grew. A substantial middle-class readership became a reality, and the demand for suitable matter continued to include plays as well as fiction, poetry, sermons, and the periodical press.[2] The new century was not even a decade old before the first multi-volume collection of Shakespeare's works appeared (1709), edited by the dramatist Nicholas Rowe. Subsequent editors such as Alexander Pope, Samuel Johnson and Edmund Malone, poets and scholars rather than playwrights, were able to address their efforts to an increasingly literate public. A homogeneous popular tradition of play-reading had developed which, by the late eighteenth century, came to include such collections as Bell's *British Theatre*, published in weekly six-penny parts, and Bell's *Shakespeare*, sold for 1s. 6d. a volume,[3] whose texts were based on the acting versions in current use at the theatres. Moreover,

---

[1] *The Spanish Fryar, or, The Double Discovery* (1681), Epistle Dedicatory.
[2] See Richard D. Altick, *The English Common Reader* (Chicago, 1957).
[3] Altick, *Common Reader*, p. 54.

audiences could purchase in the playhouse itself the text of the piece they saw performed. An avid interest in printed plays now went hand in hand with a traditionally large appetite for plays in performance.

As the century neared its end, however, a fragmentation was occurring in what had been up to this time a unified attitude towards the drama. The changing nature of the playhouse audience, the enlargement of stages and auditoriums, and the consequently greater emphasis on spectacle at the cost of the spoken word seemed to be rendering the theatre less well suited for renewing the vitality of a dramatic heritage through frequent, intelligent performance. Reading plays was becoming an alternative to playgoing instead of its happy complement. In fact, a contrary and ultimately independent tradition of dramatic appreciation had developed, one in which the individual mind, an 'audience of one', could apply itself to the permanent features of dramatic texts without paying any heed to their contemporary presentation on the stage of the living but, in the opinion of some, moribund theatre.

Among critics of the early nineteenth-century theatre the principal spokesman for this point of view was Charles Lamb, and the principal case in point was Shakespeare. Lamb's well-known essay 'On the Tragedies of Shakspeare, Considered with Reference to Their Fitness for Stage Representation' contrasts the experience of Shakespeare in the theatre with what was to Lamb the far greater satisfaction of reading the plays in the solitude of his study. Appreciative as Lamb could be of the delights of playgoing, memorably documented in the pages of his *Essays of Elia* and elsewhere, he perceived a categorical difference in Shakespeare. Seeing the character of King Lear impersonated on the stage produces the common sympathy we feel for any fellow creature, Lamb argued, but the true essence of the character can be realized only in another dimension:

The Lear of Shakspeare cannot be acted. The contemptible machinery by which they mimic the storm which he goes out in, is not more inadequate to represent the horrors of the real elements, than any actor can be to represent Lear. . . . On the stage we see nothing but corporal infirmities and weakness, the impotence of rage; while we read it, we see not Lear, but we are Lear,—we are in his mind, we are sustained by a grandeur which baffles the malice of daughters and storms. . . .[4]

Lamb's essay, and the point of view it represents, have been often explained as merely the reaction of a sensitive man to the (alleged) crudity and inappropriateness of contemporary stagecraft, but the issue is more fundamental than this. What Lamb is really getting at is the relationship between the overt action presented on the stage of a theatre and the ultimate source of that action in the human psyche. His contention is that Shakespeare, more than any other playwright, infuses complex psychological vitality into his dramatic characters and that consequently the theatre, limited to what the eye and ear may perceive, can do no real justice to the imaginative comprehensiveness of his creations.

Even if Lamb's attitude were peculiar to him alone it would require assessment, but in fact it was far more widespread. Behind it lay the association of Shakespeare's plays with developments in philosophical psychology and psychological criticism extending well back into the eighteenth century. As early as 1759 Adam Smith had propounded a doctrine of behaviour grounded on the sympathetic tendencies of human nature. His book, *The Theory of Moral Sentiments*, was frequently reprinted during the next half-century and had an undoubted influence on the Shakespearean critical tradition developing at this time. William Richardson, Thomas Whately and other late eighteenth-century writers followed Smith's precedent in concentrating on analysis of the motives that spur human beings to act, often pathetically against their own best interests and society's moral laws. In doing so, it seemed to them natural to turn to Shakespeare for models to elucidate. As Shakespeare's reputation grew in the course of the eighteenth century, his characters appeared more and more to display to the careful reader as full a range of motives and mental

[4] 'On the Tragedies of Shakspeare', *Reflector*, 4 (1812), in Lamb, I, 107.

processes as human nature itself. These studies of dramatic character resulted in a widely held fundamental agreement. No human act, these critics concluded, is explicable apart from an understanding of the mental and emotional processes that precede and cause it. Moreover, they came to hold that critical penetration into the springs of human conduct was itself a sympathetic act rendering conventional moral judgements irrelevant. Whether he could have acknowledged it or not, then, Lamb was writing in exactly this tradition when he explained in his essay on Shakespeare's tragedies that the playwright's characters 'are so much the objects of meditation rather than of interest or curiosity as to their actions, that while we are reading any of his great criminal characters,—Macbeth, Richard, even Iago,—we think not so much of the crimes which they commit, as of the ambition, the aspiring spirit, the intellectual activity, which prompts them to overleap. those moral fences'.[5]

Lamb's view is evidence for the contemporary idealization of Shakespeare that came to be called 'Bardolatry', an important phenomenon both on stage and off. But Shakespeare's plays and the attitude they fostered were, in the present context, symptomatic of an even more important shift in cultural assumptions and interests that brought about the profoundly dichotomous understanding of human nature implicit in Lamb's discussion. Apparently, this change had begun simultaneously in the theatre itself and outside it. Readers like Lamb, Coleridge and, to a lesser degree, Hazlitt found themselves put off by what less perspicacious playgoers took as the lucid, straightforward simplicity of action on the stage, and they began to say so in ever more strident voices. Certainly it was true that, following the phenomenal growth of theatres at the end of the eighteenth century, acting styles had changed in the direction of larger, less subtle gesture and louder, less finely modulated speech—developments hardly calculated to engage a class of auditors relatively unimpressed with pageantry and show. Surely, the egress from the theatre of certain segments of the playgoing public can be explained, to a

[5] Lamb, I, 106.

degree, by what they themselves might have called their more educated tastes. Especially by the time of the O.P. Riots, turning the pages of Malone's *Shakespeare* or even Bell's *British Theatre* in the leisure and privacy of one's closet must have seemed preferable to enduring rowdy, vociferous audiences, vain and sometimes intemperate players, and managements apparently bent on pandering to the popular will.

In another area as well, significant change in ideas of dramatic character had emerged. Shakespeare's plays were not the only means of entertainment or enlightenment for those who had abandoned the theatre, or had never attended it, but who still found intellectual or moral sustenance in dramatic literature. The same cultural developments that produced new generations of play readers in the late eighteenth century had also produced a new sort of playwright, who had just as resolutely turned his back on the stage or else aspired to a classical mode outside the conventions of current performed drama. In either case his example was evidence of the same widening division of sensibility.

The orientation of some of these playwrights' works, early and late in the period, is unambiguously towards the private reader. Horace Walpole's *The Mysterious Mother* (1768), printed on his own private press at Strawberry Hill, is one of the earliest examples in the genre of Gothic drama.[6] The implication of incest in the subject matter, which may strike modern readers as lurid or, as Walpole handles it, highly entertaining, would have prevented performance in the playwright's day even if he had had any thought of it. Unfortunately, very few of these 'closet' dramas can match the quality of Walpole's economically written, well-paced play. Most were likely to be of the sort illustrated by Thomas Maurice's *Panthea, or The Captive Bride* (1789), founded on a story in Xenophon. A blank-verse tragedy, *Panthea* emulates classical English drama in form and characterization, but the result is only lifeless imitation: Dryden, Lee and Rowe distilled in a theatrical vacuum. Jane West's *Edmund, Surnamed Ironside*

[6] See Evans, *Gothic Drama*.

(York, 1791), written from a similar perspective on dramatic art, reveals a more overt 'Romantic' tendency. The play provides a straightforward history of the struggle for political power in Anglo-Saxon times, the King beset by faction within and invasion without; but many of the scenes serve what is evidently the author's more compelling purpose of illustrating the private emotional conditions of her characters.

This concern with states of universalized passion is one shared by much of the produced and unproduced drama of the age. Despite the often sizeable debt of closet dramatists to earlier playwrights, their concept of human nature and its relationship to dramatic character coincides with that of writers for the contemporary stage. The obvious difference, of course, and a large one, is a lack of theatricality, an unsuitability for performance. Often this results simply from poor craftsmanship but just as often from the author's disinclination to clarify human motives by showing how they issue in action. A pronounced introspective quality obtrudes in such plays as Walter Savage Landor's *Count Julian* (1812) and Thomas Lovell Beddoes' *The Brides' Tragedy* (1822), the offshoot of a preoccupation with psychological analysis and an ignorance of the shaping limits of dramatic structure, or of a refusal to be bound by them.

Despite the difficulty of writing competently, an important aspect of the subject is the sheer number of attempts in this period to compose poetic drama. In addition to Landor and Beddoes, other, more minor literary figures tried their hands. In the early years of the period John Bidlake, Sophia Burrell, Robert Dallas, Charles Denis, James Hurdis, Mark Meilan and others all wrote unproduced tragedies; after 1800 'Barry Cornwall' (Bryan Waller Procter), George Darley, Preston Fitzgerald, Henry Grover, Frederick Howard (Earl of Carlisle), Charles Lloyd, Sarah Richardson and William Sotheby ranked among a larger group of aspiring dramatists, most of them now utterly unknown, almost all of whose plays remained unproduced.[7] Charles Lamb, Robert Southey and William Blake wrote at least one verse tragedy, as did Wordsworth.

[7] See Nicoll, III and IV, handlists.

Coleridge's output was more considerable, for, after collaborating with Southey on *The Fall of Robespierre* (1794), he composed a tragedy, *Osorio* (later produced as *Remorse*) and another, *The Death of Wallenstein* (1800). John Keats's collaboration with his friend Charles Brown resulted in his sole play, *Otho the Great*, written in 1818, and Shelley produced only one considerable drama, *The Cenci* (1819). Lord Byron, however, whose interest in the theatre was more extensive than that of any other major Romantic poet, wrote some eight plays, of which the best known are *Manfred* (1817), *Marino Faliero, Doge of Venice* (1821), *Sardanapalus* (1821) and *Werner* (1823). Five of his dramatic compositions were produced on London patent theatre stages but only one, *Marino Faliero*, within his own lifetime.

Most of the dramas represented by these authors may rest undisturbed in the near-oblivion quickly achieved on publication, but a certain few require renewed discussion. The plays of the major Romantic poets have been widely read, but largely out of duty. Indignantly rejected by some theatre historians, they have often proved no more than a source of embarrassment to literary critics. Such responses, however questionable or justified, have had the effect of shelving a body of work that not only illuminates the dramatic art of this period but elucidates moral values and philosophical ideas characteristic of the age itself.

Conventional judgement has it that, except for Keats's *Otho the Great*, Wordsworth's *The Borderers* is the weakest of these dramas. Admittedly, there is something to be said for this view. Wordsworth's sense of dramatic climax is consistently defective, where it appears at all, and his handling of certain characters, even those as important as the heroine, Idonea, is clumsy and uninspired. Moreover, the verse is sometimes wooden, often syntactically involuted. And yet the play rewards the persistent reader, who discovers in the thickets of its structure a relentless analysis of moral depravity. While it seems quite possible that Wordsworth could have made a fine narrative poem out of his materials, he seems to have perceived special advantages in dramatic form. Foremost of these, 167 perhaps, was the opportunity it offered of presenting an on-going process, for the essence of his plot is the perverse attempt of a self-made villain, Oswald, to seduce into irrevocable evil an innocent young man, Marmaduke, by exploiting his victim's keen sense of injustice. In addition, the events of the play form a logical climax to a long, vague period before them in which, the exposition informs us, Oswald floundered about in a sort of moral neutrality, bent by every wind that blew.

Regrettably, Wordsworth was unable to submit his subtle understanding of the evolution of moral and immoral character to the stringent demands of a five-act dramatic structure. Consequently the character of Oswald, Wordsworth's central figure, is opaque, blurred; what he says and does offers only fitful glimmerings of what he is. The best insight into the character as a whole occurs in the poet's Preface, written at the time of composition in 1796–97. There, as Wordsworth himself later recalled, he summed up 'those tendencies of human nature which make the apparently *motiveless* actions of bad men intelligible to careful observers'.[8] To Wordsworth, the ineluctable qualities of human nature bear no simple correlation to the events of life. He posits 'a young man of great intellectual powers yet without any solid principles of genuine benevolence'. Without such a foundation, the subject becomes the prey of all he meets and is soon betrayed into serious crime.[9]

The ultimate irony of Wordsworth's attempt at dramaturgy emerges in these remarks, since the very principle on which he founds his analysis of human nature is anti-dramatic. The commission of heinous crime has always held great dramatic fascination—witness the deeds of Clytemnestra, Herod and Jack the Ripper—but the truth Wordsworth perceives is that merely the slightest external impetus will lead such a mind as Oswald's 'to the commission of the greatest enormities'.[10] It is hardly surprising, then, that readers of *The Borderers* find the

[8] Note dictated in 1843, in *The Poetical Works of William Wordsworth*, ed. E. de Selincourt (Oxford, 1940, repr. 1963), p. 343.

[9] *Poetical Works*, p. 345.

[10] *Poetical Works*, p. 347.

conduct of its dramatic action by turns arbitrary and obscure. And yet it retains some inherent interest. Self-defensively, Wordsworth maintained that Covent Garden's rejection of a curtailed version of the play caused him no disappointment.[11] To some the play now seems only a regrettable miscalculation. Less harshly judged, it is a precocious but inexperienced young poet's attempt to define, within the unyielding conventions of Schilleresque *Sturm und Drang* drama, the permanent condition of the human heart.

Like Wordsworth, Coleridge spent considerable effort on dramatic composition in the 1790s and had a rejection by Covent Garden to show for his pains. Unlike his fellow poet and friend, Coleridge persevered and finally succeeded in having a revision of his early play *Osorio* accepted for production at Drury Lane in 1813 under the title of *Remorse*. Coleridge found the writing of plays an uncongenial discipline; yet his principal aid in these uncharacteristic exertions was his own critical sense of the nature of dramatic art, arguably the most subtle and profound of his age. Developed to a great extent through inspection of Shakespeare's plays, this critical sensitivity to the relationship between motive and act stood the aspiring playwright in good stead in attempting to adapt his 'Idea' of human nature to conventions of latter-day English tragedy, conventions he perceived to extend back through a long repertory tradition to the sensationalism and emotional extremism of the Jacobean private theatre.[12]

In placing essential human attributes within specific tragic form, Coleridge eventually came to recognize the debilitating tendencies of closet drama notably illustrated in the plays of his contemporary, Joanna Baillie. At about the same time that he was at work on the original *Osorio*, his fellow dramatist was publishing the first of her three series of *Plays on the Passions*, as they are usually called.[13] Baillie's work sheds considerable light on Coleridge's, and the fact that her view of the relationship

[11] *Poetical Works*, p. 343.
[12] See Donohue, *Dramatic Character*, pp. 13–17ff.
[13] *A Series of Plays: In Which it is Attempted to Delineate the Stronger Passions of the Mind. Each Passion Being the Subject of A Tragedy and A Comedy* (1798).

between human nature and action is closely similar to his and Wordsworth's suggests the presence of a burgeoning cultural preoccupation. The problem with most contemporary theatrical production, Baillie insisted in her long 'Introductory Discourse', is that it presents the hero only in emotional climax and so inevitably concentrates too exclusively on events. These qualities violate the traditional generic purity of the tragic form, whose object, she maintained, is to reveal the human mind 'under the dominion of those strong and fixed passions, which, seemingly unprovoked by outward circumstances, will from small beginnings brood within the breast, till all the better dispositions, all the fair gifts of nature are borne down before them'. . . .[14] One wonders if Baillie could have read Aeschylus or Seneca with any attention at all. In any case, whatever promise her theory may have held, the exemplary plays that followed form a disappointing anticlimax. The first work in Baillie's initial volume, *De Monfort*, proved a failure at Drury Lane in 1800, and the sporadic stage production of a few other works in later years does not really call in question the essentially untheatrical nature of her dramaturgy, which predictably suffers from a lack of cohesiveness between thought and deed.

The problems Coleridge encountered in dramatizing the scenario for *Osorio*, whose Moorish setting has the Spanish Inquisition as background, brought him squarely up against the implications of Baillie's concept of a deeply subjective human nature. Disarmingly, in the Preface to the manuscript sent to Drury Lane in 1797 Coleridge confessed that the central character's growth 'is nowhere explained—and yet I had most clear and psychologically accurate ideas of the whole of it'.[15] Coleridge's need was to construct a drama designed to protract over five acts the refusal of his villain-hero Osorio to feel remorse for having arranged his younger brother Albert's assassination. Initially, after its rejection by Drury Lane, Coleridge abandoned *Osorio* out of a conviction that his play

[14] Pp. 30–31.
[15] *The Complete Poetical Works of Samuel Taylor Coleridge*, ed. E. H. Coleridge (Oxford, 1912), II, 519.

could not elucidate the apparently permanent 'atrocious guilt' whose causes lay deep in the past and were now sealed up in Osorio's mind.[16]

Subsequently, however, he returned to the task of reconciling the uncharted processes of mental life with the needs of a theatrical audience. Comparison of the early *Osorio* with its 1813 revision, *Remorse*, reveals the surprising extent of improvement Coleridge effected. The haphazard plot of the original has been clarified, the main characters have emerged more sharply individuated yet psychologically well sustained, and the language has gained atmospheric power. Moreover, the specific change in the tragic ending of the play, in which the central character (now named Ordonio) is killed on stage in direct and fearful retribution for his slaughter of a henchman, involves no compromise with Coleridge's original plan to delineate the consequences of mental perversion. The modest success of the play in the theatre suggests that the general untheatricality of the plays of the Romantic poets has made for a reputation not consistently well deserved. The serious flaws that do exist in the plays of Wordsworth, Keats and others seem as much the result of their authors' disinclination to learn the craft they attempted to practise as of any more subtle malaise.

Yet the most important and well-written play of the entire group is the product of a poet who found the theatre highly distasteful and who refused to be bound by current theatrical practice. It seems promising in itself that Shelley tailored his tragedy of *The Cenci* specifically to the talents of Edmund Kean and Eliza O'Neil,[17] whose stars were both in the ascendant at the time of composition in 1819. But Kean was a fixture at Drury Lane, Miss O'Neil was jealously guarded by Covent Garden, and the characters of Count Cenci and his daughter Beatrice for which Shelley intended them established a subject of incest inadmissible in the theatre of his day. Shelley's ideals perhaps prevented him from realizing that the play would be

[16] *Works of Coleridge*, II, 519.
[17] *The Complete Poetical Works of Percy Bysshe Shelley*, ed. Thomas Hutchinson (1905, repr. 1965), p. 337.

rejected out of hand by Covent Garden even though submitted anonymously by a trusted friend. Yet the curious fact about *The Cenci* is the degree to which Shelley appears to have mastered the techniques of Romantic tragedy observable on the stage of his day. For example, the similarity of his heroine, Beatrice, to the distressed Bianca of Henry Hart Milman's *Fazio* (Covent Garden, February 1812), one of the very few plays Shelley ever went to the theatre to see, underscores both writers' extensive reliance on pathetic irony of character, unfolded in a series of situations in which an innocent female is betrayed by the unexpected emergence of situations over which she has no control.

The difference, nevertheless, between the heroines, and the plays, of Milman and Shelley does not lie entirely in Shelley's impressive intuition of Romantic and Gothic dramaturgy. Where Bianca—played in the Covent Garden production by Miss O'Neil with wonderfully telling effect—is merely pitiable, Shelley's Beatrice is a woman of miraculous fortitude of soul and vigour of intellect, finally induced through circumstances into committing a deed that, Shelley believes, cannot be fairly judged in any human tribunal. Driven past the point of temperance by psychological assault and, ultimately, physical rape perpetrated by her demonic father Count Cenci, Beatrice hires assassins who succeed in doing away with him. Arrested and brought to trial, she presents an eloquent but ultimately ambiguous argument for her own innocence. In a courtroom scene that ranks as possibly the highest achievement of Romantic poetic drama, Shelley brings to a climax the insoluble conflict of elemental good and evil, cast in the aspect of a radically innocent human being forced to act, inevitably for the worse, in a world where no good resides, where human justice proves a shallow mockery of the ideals it professes to serve.

Although certainly it was not part of Shelley's explicit plan, *The Cenci* recapitulates the essential problem faced by the Romantic poets in attempting to establish, or in refusing to accommodate, the relationship between private reality and the observed world of human action. Where Wordsworth and others had complained that the objectivity of dramatic form imposed unacceptable limitations on the presentation of human psychology, Shelley discovered a thematic analogy in the play itself, and so rendered that same objection in human terms. As he saw it, the justness of any human act depends on motives privately apprehended; consequently an unbridgeable gulf lies between the reality of any human deed as viewed by its agent and by those set up by public authority to judge it. Perceiving a chasm separating the individual from society as a whole, both Beatrice and Shelley himself find it impossible to plead her innocence effectively in a court of law. Like Wordsworth, Coleridge and Keats, Shelley had hoped to engage a public audience, but at the same time he despaired of finding spectators sympathetic to the ideals his play espoused. His presentation of human innocence stranded in an imperfect world would have been intimately familiar to Drury Lane or Covent Garden playgoers, but Shelley correctly sensed how outraged they would be by Beatrice's specific denial of guilt in the face of insurmountable 'objective' evidence to the contrary. It may be argued that it is impossible for a playwright to compose an effective tragedy aimed at an audience for whom he feels nothing other than dislike and mistrust.

The Cenci is a compelling poetic drama, then, despite a fundamental dichotomy in its point of view and in the values it attempts to elucidate. The problem was not Shelley's alone. More so than any deficiency in theatricality, this ambivalence is what divided the theatrical writing of the late eighteenth and early nineteenth centuries into dramatic poems and prosaic plays. Arguably, the dramatic compositions of these, as of all playwrights, aspire to some sort of production, whether the ideal realizable only in Charles Lamb's study or the palpable, sometimes all too concrete reality encountered in London theatres. Partly, however, because of the large changes in audiences observed by persons sensitive to the loss of subtlety and nuance in art, it became impossible for some to address their work straightforwardly to common humanity. As Byron explained in the Preface to his play *Marino Faliero*, 'The trampling of an intelligent or of an ignorant audience on a

173

production which, be it good or bad, has been a mental labour to the writer, is a palpable and immediate grievance, heightened by a man's doubt of their competency to judge, and his certainty of his own imprudence in electing them his judges. Were I capable of writing a play which could be deemed stageworthy, success would give me no pleasure, and failure great pain.'[18]

Byron has been wrongly dismissed as a dilletante for holding this point of view, although it is true that the various productions of his plays beginning as early as 1821 were not the result of his own conscious effort to write for the stage. More important, Byron's self-conscious disorientation as a playwright was by no means attributable to a sensitive personality alone. His best known play, *Manfred* (published in 1817), while obviously intended for private reading and by all odds unsuited for production, emerges out of the most influential stage tradition of the half-century before Byron wrote, the Gothic drama. Clearly, Byron's dramatization of the latter life of a morose young man consumed by unspecified guilt looks towards the practical theatre while simultaneously addressing the private reader. In fact, the play was performed, in an unauthoritative, grossly altered version, at Covent Garden in October of 1834. The plain fact is that the tragic stage and the study together faced backwards towards a former golden age but did so from the bleak promontory of a disaffected present. Even so eminently pragmatic a dramatist as M. G. Lewis saw no choice but to recognize the mutually exclusive nature of the theatre and the closet despite the highly clouded sense of genre displayed by plays written for either demesne. Regarding his single best dramatic work, *Alfonso, King of Castile*, written right at the turn of the century, Lewis confessed to grave doubts whether a blank-verse tragedy, and all that this implied, would succeed at the present time on the stage, especially after the cold response accorded *De Monfort*. 'I therefore wish this production,' he said, 'to be considered as a dramatic poem'....[19]

18 *Marino Faliero, Doge of Venice* (1821), Preface, p. xviii.
19 Lewis, *Alfonso, King of Castile*, 2nd edn. (1802), Preface, p. vi.

The ending of *Alfonso* was changed for performance at Covent Garden, but the issue it raised remained unaltered. Throughout the century that followed, and even into our own, the sort of composition Lewis resigned himself to as a 'dramatic poem' continued to be written and, to all appearances, read, while the theatre, in some respects as anaemic as the verse drama that had broken with it, continued to lament the loss of substantial numbers of the playgoing public. Certainly there were other causes of this sad division of literature and the stage, not the least of which was the extensive influx of French plays, which could be quickly translated by journeyman dramatists or free-lance hacks and bought by theatre managers for a fraction of the cost of obtaining native English drama from reputable and conscientious playwrights. Whatever the various reasons for the split, the drama has never quite regained all the audiences it lost. And it was only in the last few years of the nineteenth century, when new laws of dramatic copyright began to confer benefit on individual dramatists, that the theatre began to emerge from the dark age of pirated plays and the minuscule print of texts decipherable only by prompters and their fellow professionals. Only then, in the works of Bernard Shaw, did the full literary vitality of English dramatic art assert itself once more.

CHAPTER TEN

The Age of Kean and its Prospects

'I do not go to those theatres because they are so large; I am not comfortable.' The remark, attributed to King George IV by the actor William Dowton, may be commonplace enough, but it speaks for the sentiments of a whole class of persons, including 'the highest characters', as Dowton called them, who for one reason or another had forsaken the traditional habitat of royalty.[1] Lack of royal patronage of the theatre in this age may indeed be taken as an index of its malaise, whose causes were, of course, not confined to the size of auditoriums. It was a difficult time altogether, and the theatre felt the burdens of hardship and uncertainty as much as any public institution. Inflation and general economic problems had taken a large toll. The possibility of reasonable profit was threatened by dwindling audiences and increasing costs. Moreover, the intricate problems of managing what was in effect two or three companies amalgamated into one made it virtually impossible to run a patent theatre with anything like efficiency.

The minor theatres had their problems too, despite the overall growth and flourishing that characterized their activity during the first three decades of the new century. For some time their chief difficulty had been to find the means of skirting the letter of the law that restricted performance to burletta. Their eventual success in this appeared in their ability to win an

[1] *Report*, Q. 1521.

audience for whom patent theatre fare was either unacceptable or simply too far from home. Just how successful they were was suggested by the loud protests of the major theatres that their ancestral rights were being infringed. Yet, ironically, both major and minor theatres depended for survival on developments in the drama that to many seemed gross departures from tradition and common sense. Even the more serious criticism of the time was unequal to the task of evaluating the new drama by considering what was meaningful and satisfying for a living audience, regardless of how it might compare with the drama of the past. In sum, there was so much unprecedented, both in degree and kind, in the events and circumstances of the early nineteenth-century English theatre that no one was really in a position to take adequate stock of it.

Historians even now have achieved only a partial overview, for in our present state of knowledge it is difficult to go beyond the most comprehensive of contemporary assessments, that of the Parliamentary Inquiry of 1832 into the causes of the decline of the drama and the question of patent rights. The findings of the Parliamentary committee chaired by Edward Bulwer ranged widely over the nature and methods of theatrical production and gave special regard to the social habits and playgoing inclinations of audiences. Clearly, the single issue that put all others in perspective was whether the traditional privilege of theatrical performance granted by royal patent ought to be rigorously upheld or abandoned in favour of a policy of *laissez faire*. Bulwer himself was a reformer advocating abolition of the old patent rights, but his view was not sufficiently endorsed by fellow M.P.s. The bill that finally achieved the eradication of patent privilege was not passed until 1843, ten years after similar legislation had failed and perhaps twenty years after the conditions of licence enabled by the 1843 legislation had in practice come into being. Undeniably, the law was lethargic, but perhaps no slower than many private or professional persons to capitulate to the ineluctable pressures of the time.

For change has never been easy to assimilate. And the age of

Kean, a period of unusually significant transition—political, economic, technological and literary, as well as theatrical—was no exception. In attempting to chronicle that age, the theatrical historian is faced with difficulties arising only partly out of the relative paucity of scholarship in the field. For his task, which like any historian's calls for both descriptive synthesis and evaluation, must be done with careful regard for the special mode of reality in which theatrical production takes place. In dealing with theatrical performance, the historian has finally to consider that it presents a reality that is simultaneously aesthetic and social. The theoretical significance of this issue has some pertinence here and may justly claim the attention of the general reader and specialist alike.

It is basic to the subject that the theatre building provides the means of contact between art and audience. Consequently, performance must be defined partly in terms of the physical structure that houses it, particularly with regard to the arrangements made for presenting the dramatic scene. English scenic art from Restoration times depended on a symmetrical representation of dramatic place. In the theatres of Davenant and Killigrew and their successors, a system of parallel wings and shuttered backings painted in perspective, running in grooves and changeable in sight of the audience, provided interior and exterior settings for plays. Theoretically there is only one point in the semi-circular or horseshoe-shaped auditorium from which the scenery and its shiftings may be seen in proper perspective, a point on a line back from the vanishing point of the scenery and traditionally coinciding with the location of the royal box (which only later was moved to the side box area). Nevertheless, while the scenic machine that occupies the stage floor and the area above and below it pays formal service to the idea of monarchy, any member of the audience may imagine, from his or her own seat, what a king's-eye view takes in. A sort of vicarious identification process would seem to be part of the traditional experience of playgoing in a theatre supported by the patronage of a monarch.

178   All the same, much of the acting in this theatre was done on

a raked forestage thrust into the auditorium well beyond the line of the proscenium arch. By and large, the actors did not play within the setting but before it. The formality of the setting itself was enlivened by the constant movement of actor and actress, continuously visible (if not uniformly audible) from all parts of the house. Moreover, the production as a whole appealed straightforwardly to an assembly whose members, ranged throughout a continuously lighted auditorium, were quite aware of their collective identity. The style of acting in these surroundings had to be frankly presentational. Restoration and eighteenth-century playgoers undoubtedly saw no risk to the 'illusion of the scene' from their own visible presence any more than from the fixed décor of the proscenium, complete with doors opening onto Tony Lumpkin's horse pond or Shrewsbury Plain. For it was a fact that exits and entrances were made through portals built into the proscenium arch itself or its side projections, as well as through any of the gaps between the parallel stage wings. Audiences apparently felt no jar at seeing an actor saunter into Hyde Park through a very substantial door, closing it audibly, perhaps, behind him. In this context, then, proscenium doors become a structural symbol of the juncture of actor and audience within a special conventional reality. They help to articulate, in symbolic visual terms, the nature of a common experience, a bond uniting art and human society.

It is evident, then, that, when change occurs in the architectural structure, the specific quality of this bond may become significantly altered. Just such a change was occurring in the early nineteenth century when the proscenium doors, which had fallen into disuse, finally began to disappear. Drury Lane lost its proscenium doors in Benjamin Wyatt's 1811 building, although doors were a part of his preliminary design of 1810.[2] Covent Garden's proscenium doors were eliminated in 1812–13, in Robert Smirke's alteration of his own 1808–9 structure.[3] The loss went apparently unlamented, since these doors had been employed in recent times only for actors'

[2] *Survey of London*, pp. 58–59 & Plates 23c, 27a.
[3] *Survey of London*, pp. 96–97 & Plates 54–55.

bows.[4] In the present perspective, this change suggests that the relationship between players and audience was also undergoing alteration. As the eighteenth century gave way to the nineteenth, a different sense of propriety, or aesthetic decorum, seems to have required players to make their entrances and exits exclusively through the wings and, subsequently, in the case of interior scenes, through practical doors in flats. Together with the increasing use of elaborate scenery and spectacular effects, this development had the result of drawing the actor upstage, more and more within the scene—a withdrawal accentuated by a noticeably receding forestage. It is not surprising to find in the new Drury Lane of 1794 that the grooves in which the movable flats ran were designed 'all of one Height', according to John Kemble, indicating the abandonment of wings of decreasing height and with this the loss of exaggerated perspective, which presumably would have clashed too much in scale with actors now moving freely over the upper stage.[5] James Boaden explained that the Drury Lane company's temporary residence at the Royal Opera House while the new theatre was being built had a crucial result. 'We were drawn by that stage,' he said, 'into a fondness for spectacle, which we could gratify, sooner than a demand for sense; and at length the people themselves preferred the great theatre to the little one.'[6]

In view of these related shifts in taste and emphasis, the abandonment of the proscenium door and the emergence of a proscenium arch resembling a picture frame seem a logical consequence. A concomitant result of these changes, however, was the loss of a certain intimacy created by the habitual use of an architectural feature at once part of the scene and part of the auditorium. Clearly, that sense of intimacy was not dependent simply on the size of the auditorium. More exactly, the disappearance of the proscenium door signals the theatre's turn from a presentational style of performance, based on acknowledged artifice, to one based on representation, on the

[4] Richard Southern, 'Proscenium', *Oxford Companion to the Theatre*, 3rd edn.
[5] Kemble's Diary, British Museum Add. MS. 31,972–5, quoted in Southern, *Changeable Scenery* (1952), p. 245.   [6] Boaden, *Life of Jordan*, I, 204.

illusion of actual life. The withdrawal of the aesthetic limit of that illusion inside the floor line of the arch itself suggests a new feeling of separateness on the part of actor and audience. That this leads to a greater identification of the actor with his role is suggested by Hazlitt's caution to actors that they ought not to sit in the boxes when witnessing a performance. Being so much on display as persons, he explains, prevents them from fully drawing the audience into their characters when on stage.[7] Hazlitt's opinion would not have been understood in an earlier age.

The precedent, then, for the completeness of scenic illusion achieved on the mid-century Victorian stage lies in developments of this kind, at once theatrical, aesthetic and social. They are scarcely apparent, perhaps, to the eyes of contemporaries. To be seen clearly, they must be studied within a relatively long span of time, in the perspective afforded by history. Such a view necessarily highlights the fact of continuity in the theatre. More evidently than in the case of any other art, theatrical or dramatic genius emerges only irregularly, and so is too uncertain a basis for broad understanding. To concentrate exclusively on pre-eminent achievement is to mistake the true nature of the medium. The best criterion is not individual genius, nor the relationship of the drama to the thought of the age, but, rather, the fundamental one of vitality. Theatrical vitality consists in the observable and continuing impact of a theatre on an audience significantly representative of the society from which it is drawn. That audience may well be other than the proverbial cross-section of the London populace that, we are taught, frequented Shakespeare's Globe. It may not exemplify the wisdom of its elders or acknowledge the aspirations of its youth. But it will share a feeling for both the passing interests and abiding concerns of its day, and will recognize and respond to their representation, however oblique, on the stage. The social implications of melodrama—to take the clearest example from the age of Kean—lend support to this notion of vitality, since melodrama attracted audiences in large numbers

[7] 'Whether Actors Ought to Sit in the Boxes', in Hazlitt, VIII, 272ff.

to both major and minor theatres by speaking, in the accents and tones of the day, of fears, desires and needs characteristic of a growing and troubled community. The departure from the theatre of a more privileged class of spectators during this time actually helps to pinpoint the source of new vitality.

Melodrama, and the nineteenth-century British theatre as a whole, are currently the subject of wide reassessment. The materials, in the form of printed and manuscript plays, playbills, programmes, memoirs, diaries, account books, reviews, promptbooks, extra-illustrated books, periodicals and the general ephemera that have grown up around the theatre, survive in unprecedented quantity and uncalculated richness. The most basic of all tasks, determining exactly what was performed before audiences, night after night throughout the century, has only begun. Meanwhile, a great deal of work on a small scale must also take place. As G. Kitson Clark has said of the materials pertaining to the history of Victorian England, the new details that appear may not seem to have been worth the trouble to unearth, since they so often relate to obscure persons, places and events that may claim at most a secondary importance. Yet it is exactly from sources like these that large changes will eventually come in our understanding of the history of that age.[8]

In view of the possibilities for new knowledge, only a tentative assessment of the theatre in the age of Edmund Kean seems appropriate. In the perspective of the present time it may appear a disappointing age. The sameness of so many of its plays is oppressive. A considerable segment of society had vacated its place in the audience. Government regulation of the theatrical enterprise espoused a reactionary attitude towards the drama and encouraged widespread violation of the law. And yet it is an exciting age, full of interest and promise. Despite professional reluctance, continued official intolerance, and the presence of habits of life and mind ill-suited to theatrical attendance and artistic appreciation, a new drama and a new audience had emerged, and new theatres had arisen

[8] G. Kitson Clark, *The Making of Victorian England* (Cambridge, Mass., 1962, repr. New York, 1967), p. 3.

to house them. At the same time, a vigorous acting tradition met and triumphed over the challenges of enlarged auditoriums and the influx of an unfamiliar and rudely vociferous clientele.

It remained for Queen Victoria to restore a measure of confidence in the social acceptability of the theatre and, by implication, in its moral efficacy. It remained also for improving standards of theatrical production, a growing sense of national identity and well-being, and an increasingly large popular audience to bring about the movement of the theatre into the mainstream of nineteenth-century life, where the common and the genteel might move towards a more happy accord.

But this was all for the future. Ultimately, the English theatre of the early nineteenth century is not important because it paved the way for the plays of Robertson and, later, of Jones, Pinero, Wilde, Shaw and Granville-Barker. On the contrary, it commands our interest on its own account. There is much in the period for all who find instruction or delight in the theatre of the past. Moreover, the abundance and complexity of the records it has left render it unusually attractive to the theatre historian, who in investigating earlier times must often be resigned to more fragmentary leavings. That it was largely an unliterary period, so far as the nature of its drama was concerned, and that most of its plays did not outlive their own time, hardly make it unusual. It is the untypical that likely becomes the classic, whereas the theatre as a whole embraces the anomalous and the normal with quite undifferentiated fervour, preoccupied as it is with the all-engrossing present. However sensitive we must be to the presence, and endurance, of great art, we must also acknowledge its inescapably quotidian origins. If the vitality of the theatre in the age of Kean remains imperfectly demonstrated, it is perhaps clear that the nature of the ongoing enterprise itself must ground our understanding first and last. For, in the final analysis, the qualities that perennially distinguish the theatre are inseparable from those that identify the spirit of the age. Or so our present perspective suggests.

Bibliography

A separate list of plays will be found in the Index. Except for a few items of marginal relevance, the following list gathers all the works cited in the text and notes. Some brief annotation is provided for items of basic scholarship. As in the Notes, the place of publication is London, unless otherwise indicated.

Actors and Actresses of Great Britain and the United States, ed. Brander Matthews and Laurence Hutton. 5 vols. New York, 1886.

Adolphus, John. *Memoirs of John Bannister, Comedian.* 2 vols. 1839.

Altick, Richard D. *The English Common Reader.* Chicago, 1957.

Arundell, Dennis. *The Story of Sadler's Wells.* 1965.

An Authentic Statement of Facts. 1818. One of numerous occasional pamphlets published in the period, this one relating to the finances of Drury Lane.

Bagster-Collins, Jeremy F. *George Colman The Younger 1762–1836.* New York, 1946.

Baker, H. Barton. *History of the London Stage and its Famous Players (1576–1903).* London and New York, 1904. Although some of its scholarship is out of date, this remains one of the basic, and most engagingly written, scholarly histories of the subject.

Baker, Herschel. *John Philip Kemble: The Actor in His Theatre.* Cambridge, Mass., 1942.

185

Ball, Robert. *The Amazing Career of Sir Giles Overreach.* Princeton, 1939.

Bishop, Conrad Joy. 'Melodramatic Acting: Concept and Technique in the Performance of Early Nineteenth Century English Melodrama.' Diss. Stanford, 1967.

Boaden, James. *The Life of Mrs. Jordan.* 2 vols. 1831.

— *Memoirs of the Life of John Philip Kemble.* 2 vols. 1825.

— *Memoirs of Mrs. Siddons.* 2 vols. 1827.

Brayley, Edward Wedlake. *Historical and Descriptive Accounts of the Theatres of London.* 1826 [for 1827].

Bulwer, Edward. *England and the English,* ed. Standish Meacham. Chicago, 1970.

Colman, George, the Younger. *Random Records.* 2 vols. 1830. The autobiography of a man who, as playwright, manager, and official examiner of plays, was one of the central and most important figures in the theatre of his age.

Covent Garden Journal, ed. J. J. Stockdale. 2 vols. 1810.

Cumberland, Richard. *Memoirs of Richard Cumberland. Written by Himself.* 2 vols. 1807.

Decastro, Jacob. *The Memoirs of J. Decastro, Comedian.* 1824.

Dibdin, Charles. *The Professional Life of Mr. Dibdin, Written by Himself.* 2 vols. 1803.

Dibdin, Charles, the Younger. *Professional & Literary Memoirs of Charles Dibdin the Younger,* ed. George Speaight. 1956.

Donohue, Joseph W., Jr. *Dramatic Character in the English Romantic Age.* Princeton, 1970. Contains an extensive bibliography of primary and secondary sources relating to the theatre of the period.

—, ed. *The Theatrical Manager in England and America.* Princeton, 1971.

Essays on Nineteenth Century British Theatre, ed. Kenneth Richards and Peter Thomson. 1971.

Evans, Bertrand. *Gothic Drama from Walpole to Shelley.* Berkeley and Los Angeles, 1947.

Fitzgerald, Percy. *The Kembles.* 1871.

— *The Life of David Garrick.* Rev. edn. 1889.

Foote, Horace. *A Companion to the Theatres; and a Manual of the British Drama.* 1829.

Genest, Rev. John. *Some Account of the English Stage.* 10 vols. Bath, 1832. Although factually outdated to 1800 by *The London Stage 1660–1800* (*q.v.*), Genest's calendar remains the fullest guide to early nineteenth-century performances on the London stage, and his comments on the plays and players of post-Restoration Britain, sometimes objective, sometimes otherwise, will never be superseded.

Ganzel, Dewey. 'Patent Wrongs and Patent Theatres: Drama and the Law in the Early Nineteenth Century.' *PMLA*, 76 (1961), pp. 386–387.

Gilliland, Thomas. *A Dramatic Synopsis.* 1804.

Hawkins, F. W. *The Life of Edmund Kean.* 1869. Extra-illustrated edition in the Harvard Theatre Collection.

Hazlitt, William. *Complete Works*, ed. P. P. Howe. 21 vols. 1930–34.

Hillebrand, H. N. *Edmund Kean.* New York, 1933. The best, most reliable biography of the actor and a model of biographical and theatrical scholarship.

Hogan, Charles Beecher. *The London Stage 1776–1800.* Carbondale, Ill., 1968. Part 5 of *The London Stage 1660–1800* (*q.v.*).

Howard, Frederick. *Thoughts on the Present Condition of the Stage, and upon the Construction of a New Theatre.* 1809.

Hughes, Leo. *The Drama's Patrons: A Study of the Eighteenth-Century London Audience.* Austin, Texas, and London, 1971.

Hunt, Leigh. *Critical Essays on the Performers of the London Theatres.* 1807.

— *Leigh Hunt's Dramatic Criticism 1808–1831*, ed. L. H. and C. W. Houtchens. New York, 1949.

Jefferson, Joseph. *The Autobiography of Joseph Jefferson*, ed. Alan S. Downer. Cambridge, Mass., 1964.

Kemble, John Philip. 'Memoranda of J. P. Kemble.' 5 vols. British Museum Add. MSS. 31,972–76.

Lamb, Charles. *The Works of Charles and Mary Lamb*, ed. E. V. Lucas. Vols. 1 and 2. 1903.

The Letters of Richard Brinsley Sheridan, ed. Cecil Price. 3 vols. Oxford, 1966.

Lewes, George Henry. *On Actors and the Art of Acting.* 1875.

The London Stage 1660–1800, ed. Emmett L. Avery, Charles Beecher Hogan, Arthur H. Scouten, George Winchester Stone, Jr., and William Van Lennep. 5 parts, 11 vols. Carbondale, Ill., 1960–68. A comprehensive calendar of daily performances on the London stage for the dates covered, this work contains basic information about the theatre of the period and is indispensable both for the facts it provides and for the standard of scholarship it sets.

Lorenzen, Richard L. 'Managers of the Old Prince of Wales's Theatre.' *Theatre Notebook*, 24 (1969), pp. 32–36.

— 'The Old Prince of Wales's Theatre.' *Theatre Notebook*, 25 (1971), pp. 132–145.

Mammen, Edward William. *The Old Stock Company School of Acting.* Boston, 1945.

Mander, Raymond, and Joe Mitchenson. *The Lost Theatres of London.* 1968.

— *The Theatres of London.* 2nd edn. 1963.

[Martin, H.] *Remarks on Mr. John Kemble's Performance of Hamlet and Richard the Third.* 1802.

Moore, Thomas. *Memoirs of the Life of the Right Honourable Richard Brinsley Sheridan.* 1825.

Nicholson, Watson. *The Struggle for a Free Stage in London.* Boston, 1906. A work of lasting scholarly importance dealing with the complex issue of theatrical licensing and its pervasive effect on the post-Restoration theatre.

Nicoll, Allardyce. *A History of English Drama 1660–1900.* 6 vols. Cambridge, 1952–59. The standard history of the subject, with extensive handlists of plays and a comprehensive title index.

Oulton, W. C. *A History of the Theatres of London.* 2 vols. 1818.

Oxberry's Dramatic Biography. 5 vols. 1825.

Price, Cecil. *The English Theatre in Wales in the Eighteenth Century.* Cardiff, 1948.

'Prologue Spoken by Mr. Garrick at the Opening of the Theatre in Drury-Lane, 1747', in R. S. Crane, ed., *A Collection of English Poems 1660–1800.* New York, 1932. Pp. 667–668.

Raymond, George. *Memoirs of Robert William Elliston*. 2 vols. 1846, repr. New York, 1969.

Rede, Leman Thomas. *The Road to the Stage*. 1827.

Report from the Select Committee on Dramatic Literature: with the Minutes of Evidence. House of Commons, 2 August 1832. One of the most significant primary documents of the period, this transcript of the committee minutes covers many important topics, including theatrical licensing, management, the acting profession, dramatic genres, and the state of the contemporary drama, and contains first-hand evidence from many persons related to the theatre.

Reynolds, Frederick. *The Life and Times of Frederick Reynolds. Written by Himself*. 2 vols. 1826.

Rosenfeld, Sybil. 'Stock Company', in *The Oxford Companion to the Theatre*. 3rd edn. 1967.

Saunders, George. *A Treatise on Theatres*. 1790.

Saxon, A. H. *Enter Foot and Horse: A History of Hippodrama in England and France*. New Haven, 1968.

Scrimgeour, Gary J. 'Drama and the Theatre in the Early Nineteenth Century.' Diss. Princeton, 1968.

Southern, Richard. *Changeable Scenery*. 1952.

— 'Proscenium', in *The Oxford Companion to the Theatre*. 3rd edn.

Sprague, Arthur Colby. *Shakespearian Players and Performances*. Cambridge, Mass., 1953.

Stone, George Winchester, Jr. 'Bloody, Cold, and Complex Richard; David Garrick's Interpretation', in *On Stage and Off*, ed. John W. Ehrstine *et al.* Pullman, Wash., 1968. Pp. 14–25.

Stratman, Carl J., C.S.V. *Britain's Theatrical Periodicals 1720–1967*. New York, 1972.

Survey of London. General ed. F. H. W. Sheppard. Vol. 35: *The Theatre Royal Drury Lane and The Royal Opera House Covent Garden*. Published for the Greater London Council. 1970. A detailed historical account of the two theatres, with primary attention given to the evolution of the physical structure and management, this superbly documented work provides a full factual history of the English patent theatre.

Taylor, Aline M. *Next to Shakespeare: Otway's* Venice Preserv'd *and* The Orphan *and Their History on the London Stage.* Durham, N.C., 1950.

Tomlins, F. G. *A Brief View of the English Drama.* 1840.

The Trial of Mr. John Palmer, Comedian, and Manager of the Royalty Theatre. 1787.

Troubridge, St. Vincent. *The Benefit System in the British Theatre.* 1967. A concise yet full examination of a practice that had a significant effect on the lives and fortunes of generations of players and managers.

INDEX

Plays and Other Performed Pieces

191

INDEX

Persons, Non-Dramatic Works and Subjects

195

monopoly, theatrical *see* patent
rights
Monthly Mirror 143
Moore, Edward 26, 69, 86
Morning Chronicle 143
Morris, D. E. 152–53, 157
Morton, Thomas 75, 76, 90–93,
128
Munden, Joseph 77, 80, 82–83; as
Old Dozey 82, 147
Murphy, Arthur 26, 86

Nash, John 32
New Olympic Theatre *see* Olympic
New Pavilion (Whitechapel) 45
New Royal Sussex Theatre 45

O'Hara, Kane 47
O'Keeffe, John 76, 87
Oliver Twist (Dickens) 120
Olivier, Laurence, as Othello 63
Olympic Pavilion (1806), also known
as Pavilion Theatre, Olympic
Saloon, Astley's Middlesex
Amphitheatre, Astley's Theatre,
New Pavilion Theatre, Theatre
Royal Pavilion (Astley's), Olympic,
New Olympic 2, 38–40
Olympic Theatre 39, 40, 131; *see also*
Olympic Pavilion
O'Neill (*or* O'Neil), Eliza 137, 171
Opie, Amelia 120
'O. P. Riots' 6, 52–55, 155, 165
Osbaldiston, David 158
Otway, Thomas 25, 85
Oulton, W. C. 108

Palmer, John 12–13, 31, 45, 49, 71
pantomime 19, 23, 33, 34, 39, 42, 51,
56, 74, 77, 78, 108, 109, 115,
128, 130
Paradoxe sur le Comédien (Diderot) 68
Parliamentary inquiry (1832) 177
et passim
patent rights 2–3, 9–10ff., 12ff.,

38, 177; *see also* burletta; theatres,
major and minor
patent theatres, in provinces 28;
see also Covent Garden; Drury
Lane
Paul, J. 44
Pavilion Theatre (Stepney) 158
Payne, John Howard 141
Pepys, Samuel 15
Philips, Ambrose 26, 86
Pilon, Frederick 74
Pinero, Arthur Wing 183
Pixérécourt, Guilbert de 106, 115
Planché, James Robinson 40
Pocock, Isaac 117–18, 119
Pope, Alexander (actor), as Othello
71
Pope, Alexander (poet and editor)
161
Powell, Mary Ann, as the castle
spectre 101
Prince of Wales's Royal Theatre 44
Procter, Bryan Waller ('Barry
Cornwall') 166
proscenium doors 179–80
Public Advertiser 143

Quin, James 62

Racine, Jean 86
Rae, Alexander 76
repertory company 72–73ff., 77–78
repertory system *see* acting
repertory theatre, idea of 20–21;
illustrated 21–26
Reynolds, Frederick 128
Richardson, Sarah 166
Richardson, William 163
riots, in the theatre 155–56; *see also*
'O. P. Riots'
Roberdeau, John Peter 24
Robertson, T. W. 44, 183
Robinson, Mary 23
Rob Roy (Scott) 119
Rodwell and Jones, purchasers of
Sans Pareil Theatre 42

199